OLIVER GOLDSMITH

Modern Critical Views

Henry Adams
Edward Albee
A. R. Ammons
Matthew Arnold
John Ashbery
W. H. Auden
Jane Austen
James Baldwin
Charles Baudelaire
Samuel Beckett
Saul Bellow
The Bible
Elizabeth Bishop
William Blake
Jorge Luis Borges
Elizabeth Bowen
Bertolt Brecht
The Brontës
Robert Browning
Anthony Burgess
George Gordon, Lord
  Byron
Thomas Carlyle
Lewis Carroll
Willa Cather
Cervantes
Geoffrey Chaucer
Kate Chopin
Samuel Taylor Coleridge
Joseph Conrad
Contemporary Poets
Hart Crane
Stephen Crane
Dante
Charles Dickens
Emily Dickinson
John Donne & the Seven-
  teenth-Century Meta-
  physical Poets
Elizabethan Dramatists
Theodore Dreiser
John Dryden
George Eliot
T. S. Eliot
Ralph Ellison
Ralph Waldo Emerson
William Faulkner
Henry Fielding
F. Scott Fitzgerald
Gustave Flaubert
E. M. Forster
Sigmund Freud
Robert Frost

Robert Graves
Graham Greene
Thomas Hardy
Nathaniel Hawthorne
William Hazlitt
Seamus Heaney
Ernest Hemingway
Geoffrey Hill
Friedrich Hölderlin
Homer
Gerard Manley Hopkins
William Dean Howells
Zora Neale Hurston
Henry James
Samuel Johnson and
  James Boswell
Ben Jonson
James Joyce
Franz Kafka
John Keats
Rudyard Kipling
D. H. Lawrence
John Le Carré
Ursula K. Le Guin
Doris Lessing
Sinclair Lewis
Robert Lowell
Norman Mailer
Bernard Malamud
Thomas Mann
Christopher Marlowe
Carson McCullers
Herman Melville
James Merrill
Arthur Miller
John Milton
Eugenio Montale
Marianne Moore
Iris Murdoch
Vladimir Nabokov
Joyce Carol Oates
Sean O'Casey
Flannery O'Connor
Eugene O'Neill
George Orwell
Cynthia Ozick
Walter Pater
Walker Percy
Harold Pinter
Plato
Edgar Allan Poe
Poets of Sensibility & the
  Sublime

Alexander Pope
Katherine Ann Porter
Ezra Pound
Pre-Raphaelite Poets
Marcel Proust
Thomas Pynchon
Arthur Rimbaud
Theodore Roethke
Philip Roth
John Ruskin
J. D. Salinger
Gershom Scholem
William Shakespeare
  (3 vols.)
  Histories & Poems
  Comedies
  Tragedies
George Bernard Shaw
Mary Wollstonecraft
  Shelley
Percy Bysshe Shelley
Edmund Spenser
Gertrude Stein
John Steinbeck
Laurence Sterne
Wallace Stevens
Tom Stoppard
Jonathan Swift
Alfred, Lord Tennyson
William Makepeace
  Thackeray
Henry David Thoreau
Leo Tolstoi
Anthony Trollope
Mark Twain
John Updike
Gore Vidal
Virgil
Robert Penn Warren
Evelyn Waugh
Eudora Welty
Nathanael West
Edith Wharton
Walt Whitman
Oscar Wilde
Tennessee Williams
William Carlos Williams
Thomas Wolfe
Virginia Woolf
William Wordsworth
Richard Wright
William Butler Yeats

These and other titles in preparation

Modern Critical Views

OLIVER GOLDSMITH

Edited and with an introduction by
Harold Bloom
Sterling Professor of the Humanities
Yale University

CHELSEA HOUSE PUBLISHERS ◇ 1987
New York ◇ New Haven ◇ Philadelphia

© 1987 by Chelsea House Publishers, a division
of Chelsea House Educational Communications, Inc.,
  95 Madison Avenue, New York, NY 10016
  345 Whitney Avenue, New Haven, CT 06511
  5068B West Chester Pike, Edgemont, PA 19028

Introduction © 1987 by Harold Bloom

Printed and bound in the United States of America

10 9 8 7 6 5 4 3 2 1

∞ The paper used in this publication meets the minimum
requirements of the American National Standard for Permanence
of Paper for Printed Library Materials, Z39.48-1984.

Library of Congress Cataloging-in-Publication Data
Oliver Goldsmith.
    (Modern critical views)
    Bibliography: p.
    Includes index.
    Summary: Essays of literary criticism on the works
of the eighteenth-century writer who engaged in a wide
variety of occupations before embarking on a literary
career.
    1. Goldsmith, Oliver, 1728–1774—Criticism and
interpretation. [1. Goldsmith, Oliver, 1728–1774—
Criticism and interpretation   2. English literature—
Irish authors—History and criticism]   I. Bloom, Harold.
II. Series.
PR3494.045   1987   828'.609   87-5188
ISBN 1-55546-281-2 (alk. paper)

Contents

Editor's Note

This book brings together the best modern criticism of Oliver Goldsmith, arranged in the chronological order of its original publication. I am grateful to Christina Büchmann for her erudite aid in editing this volume.

My introduction centers upon *The Vicar of Wakefield* as a revision of the Book of Job, and *She Stoops to Conquer* as a Freudian farce before Freud. Ronald Paulson begins the chronological sequence of criticism by placing the *Vicar* in the context of the novel of manners, from Fielding through Austen, while R. F. Brissenden provocatively contrasts Burchell with Primrose, and illuminates the way in which Goldsmith sentimentally forces the happy ending on the book.

Wayne C. Booth strongly presents *The Citizen of the World* as a self-portrait of Goldsmith's genius, and so as his most important work. In another strong reading, Oliver W. Ferguson analyzes both *The Good Natur'd Man* and *She Stoops to Conquer* as parodies of the sentimental drama of Goldsmith's century.

Roger Lonsdale, the definitive editor of Goldsmith's poetry, gives an informed account of his major poems in the context of the Age of Pope. Whereas my introduction sees the *Vicar* as Goldsmith's essentially personal revision of Job, James H. Lehmann learnedly traces the effect upon the novel of contemporary scholarship dominated by Lowth, a perspective that secularized, primitivized, and "Orientalized" the Hebrew Bible.

Charles A. Knight returns us to *The Citizen of the World*, supplementing Booth's classic study, while C. C. Barfoot on *The Deserted Village* and Pat Rogers on *The Traveller* adumbrate aspects of the poems that Lonsdale introduced for us. *She Stoops to Conquer* is considered briefly by Bernard Harris, after which Thomas R. Preston concludes this volume with a reading of the *Vicar* that contextualizes it in eighteenth-century biblical criticism, as Lehmann does, while using the context to deny recent critical approaches that would degrade the Vicar from his Jobean status.

Introduction

Oliver Goldsmith, versatile and graceful in every genre, compels a critic to speculate upon the disproportion between the writer-as-person and the writer-as-writer. Some (not all) of the most accomplished writers I have known have been the most colorless of personalities, or if more vivid and interesting as people, then they have been remarkably unpleasant or foolish or merely mawkish. Goldsmith appears to have been a luckless individual and even what Freud called a "moral masochist," a victim of his own death-drive at the age of forty-four. Indeed, Goldsmith is a fairly classic instance of many Freudian insights, and both *The Vicar of Wakefield* and *She Stoops to Conquer* sustain immediate illumination when Freudian categories are applied to them. What Freud termed "the most prevalent form of degradation in erotic life" is a clear guide to young Marlow's backwardness with well-born women, and exuberant aggressivity with inn barmaids, college bedmakers, and others of whom he remarks: "They are of *us* you know." And the lumpish Tony Lumpkin becomes an even more persuasive representation when his descent into the company of the alehouse is seen, again in Freudian guise, as a reaction-formation to his dreadful mother, Mrs. Hardcastle.

Goldsmith aped Johnson in most things, even to the copying of the critic's manner, according to Boswell. Johnson spoke the last word upon his friend and follower: "If nobody was suffered to abuse poor Goldy but those who could write as well, he would have few censors." Yet it is a curious sadness that the best lines in any poem by Goldsmith, the concluding passage of *The Deserted Village,* were written by Johnson himself:

> That trade's proud empire hastes to swift decay,
> As ocean sweeps the laboured mole away;

> While self-dependent power can time defy,
> As rocks resist the billows and the sky.

An ironical reading might interpret that humanly constructed break-water, "the laboured mole," as Goldsmith's ego, in contrast to Johnsonian self-dependence, the great critic's rock-like ego. Still, Goldsmith's laboured breakwater has defied time also, though not quite with the massive Johnsonian force. Goldsmith's writing survives on its curious grace, curious both because it resists strict definition and because it extends across the genres: from the Popean verse of *The Traveller,* through the Bunyanesque revision of the Book of Job in the sentimental novel *The Vicar of Wakefield,* on to the elegiac pastoralism of *The Deserted Village,* the permanently successful stage comedy *She Stoops to Conquer,* and the urbane good nature of the posthumously published poem *Retaliation,* a gentle satire upon the members of Dr. Johnson's Club.

The strongest case for Goldsmith was made by William Hazlitt, second only to Johnson in my estimate, among all critics in the language:

> Goldsmith, both in verse and prose, was one of the most delight-
> ful writers in the language. . . . His ease is quite unconscious.
> Everything in him is spontaneous, unstudied, yet elegant, har-
> monious, graceful, nearly faultless.

A kind of natural or unconscious artist, Goldsmith prevails by disarm-ing his reader. He seems the least tendentious of all authors, writing as though he had no design upon us. Even now he has not lost his audience, although critics sometimes treat his works as period pieces. He is strangely close to popular literature, though he hardly can sustain comparison with the far more powerful Bunyan. Perhaps he moves us now primarily as an instance of our continuity with a past that we seem otherwise wholly to have abandoned.

II

The canonical status of *The Vicar of Wakefield* is beyond doubt, though I do not advise rereading it side by side with Bunyan's far stronger *The Pilgrim's Progress* as I have just done. But then, Bunyan is so powerful a visionary as to claim the company of Milton and Blake. Goldsmith gives us a gentle theodicy in the *Vicar,* and theodicy is hardly a gentle mode. Henry James, writing an introduction to the novel in 1900, called it "the spoiled child of our literature," a work so amiable that it seemed to him "happy in the manner in which a happy man is happy — a man, say, who has married an angel or been appointed to a sinecure."

Like the Book of Job, the *Vicar* brings a good man, here Dr. Primrose, into the power of Satan, here Squire Thornhill. Some recent revisionist readings of the *Vicar* have attempted to give us a Dr. Primrose who is more self-righteous than virtuous, more smugly egoistical than innocent. These seem to me weak misreadings because they overlook Goldsmith's most surprising revision of the Book of Job. With singular audacity, Goldsmith makes his Job the narrator. Whatever you have Job do, you ought not to make him the hero of a first-person narrative. Consider the aesthetic and spiritual effect that even the opening would then have upon us:

> I was a man in the land of Uz, and my name was Job; I was perfect and upright, and I feared God, and eschewed evil.

No one proclaims his own virtues without alienating us, and no one recites his own sufferings without embarrassing us. The opening of *The Vicar of Wakefield* is not quite like that of a first-person Book of Job, but it is problematic enough:

> I was ever of opinion, that the honest man who married and brought up a large family, did more service than he who continued single and only talked of population. From this motive, I had scarce taken orders a year, before I began to think seriously of matrimony, and chose my wife, as she did her wedding-gown, not for a fine glossy surface, but such qualities as would wear well.

At best, poor Primrose sounds a pompous fool; at worst, a bore rampant. Why did Goldsmith take the risk? Was Primrose intended to be a satiric butt and Burchell a reality instructor? Dickens evidently did not think so, and something of Primrose got into Mr. Pickwick. Unlike Goethe and Dickens, we do not find Primrose to be altogether comically lovable. However, we also ought not to fault him. Perhaps he does represent a secularization of the figure of Job or a Johnsonian allegory of an education in true humility, but I suspect that he is primarily Goldsmith's introjection of Job. This is not to suggest a composite figure, Job/Primrose-Goldsmith as it were, but to intimate that Primrose is a loving self-satire on Goldsmith's part, or an amiable Jobean parody directed against the feckless writer's own penchant for catastrophe.

Goldsmith takes the risk of first-person narration because he knows that the Vicar Primrose is his own somewhat ironic self-portrait and that his

personal Jobean tribulations do not exactly achieve sublimity. Yet Goldsmith, in life, and the Vicar, in the novel, cannot refrain from self-praise,
from a kind of snobbery of virtue, even as they are altogether the passive
victims of fortune. Goldsmith, though an impossible personality, was a
literary genius, but Dr. Primrose is simply not very clever. An unintelligent
Job startles us, if only by reminding us what a formidable moral psycholo-
gist and reasoner the biblical Job was, so much so that he finally infuriated
John Calvin, his greatest commentator. Calvin, in his sermons on the Book
of Job, is finally provoked to cry out that God would have had to make new
worlds to satisfy Job. No one would say that God would have had to make
new worlds to satisfy Dr. Primrose. Goldsmith himself, I suspect, was about
halfway between Job and the Vicar in this regard.

III

The Citizen of the World, The Vicar of Wakefield, and the three major
poems may be the best of Goldsmith, but I myself prefer *She Stoops to
Conquer.* It has held the stage for more than two hundred years and may
well be the authentic instance of a popular drama in English after
Shakespeare. Though it was intended as a parody upon what Goldsmith
called Sentimental as opposed to Laughing Comedy, we have lost the satire
without losing the value of the work. It remains very funny and evidently
always will be funny. Goldsmith did not intend farce, but that is what *She
Stoops to Conquer* assuredly is: major farce. There is something Shakespearean about Kate Hardcastle, though to compare her to the Rosalind of
As You Like It is an offence against literary tact, as is any comparison of
Tony Lumpkin to Puck.

Goldsmith had the literary good sense to keep his farce simple, reduc-
tive, and almost primitive; the portrait of Mrs. Hardcastle has a kind of
unrelenting savagery about it. And Tony Lumpkin's ordeal-by-fright for her
is not less than sadistic, with a cruelty in which we are compelled to share:

> TONY. Never fear me. Here she comes. Vanish. She's got from the
> pond, and draggled up to the waist like a mermaid.
> *Enter Mrs Hardcastle.*
> MRS HARDCASTLE. Oh, Tony, I'm killed. Shook. Battered to death.
> I shall never survive it. That last jolt that laid us against the
> quickset hedge has done my business.
> TONY. Alack, mama, it was all your own fault. You would be for
> running away by night, without knowing one inch of the
> way.

MRS HARDCASTLE. I wish we were at home again. I never met so many accidents in so short a journey. Drenched in the mud, overturned in a ditch, stuck fast in a slough, jolted to a jelly, and at last to lose our way. Whereabouts do you think we are, Tony?

TONY. By my guess we should be upon Crack-skull Common, about forty miles from home.

MRS HARDCASTLE. O lud! O lud! the most notorious spot in all the country. We only want a robbery to make a complete night on't.

TONY. Don't be afraid, mama, don't be afraid. Two of the five that kept here are hanged, and the other three may not find us. Don't be afraid. Is that a man that's galloping behind us? No; it's only a tree. Don't be afraid.

MRS HARDCASTLE. The fright will certainly kill me.

TONY. Do you see anything like a black hat moving behind the thicket?

MRS HARDCASTLE. O death!

TONY. No, it's only a cow. Don't be afraid, mama; don't be afraid.

MRS HARDCASTLE. As I'm alive, Tony, I see a man coming towards us. Ah! I'm sure on't. If he perceives us we are undone.

TONY (aside). Father-in-law, by all that's unlucky, come to take one of his night walks. (To her) Ah, it's a highwayman, with pistols as long as my arm. A damned ill-looking fellow.

MRS HARDCASTLE. Good heaven defend us! He approaches.

TONY. Do you hide yourself in that thicket, and leave me to manage him. If there be any danger I'll cough and cry, Hem! When I cough be sure to keep close.
Mrs Hardcastle hides behind a tree in the Back Scene.

To find a comparable savagery, one would have to turn to W. S. Gilbert. There is a touch of Gilbert to *She Stoops to Conquer*, if only because we are already in that cosmos of nonsense that is shadowed by the Freudian reality principle. Freud, writing on "Humor" in 1928, heard in it the voice of the super-ego, speaking "kindly words of comfort to the intimidated ego." This does not take us far when we consider Shakespearean comedy at its most complex, *As You Like It* or *All's Well That Ends Well*. But it beautifully enlightens us as to Goldsmith's holiday from the superego in *She Stoops to Conquer*. Goldsmith was very uncomfortable as Job, even as that most amiable and silly of Jobs, Dr. Primrose. But he was supremely comfortable as Tony Lumpkin, his kindly word of comfort to his own intimidated ego.

RONALD PAULSON

The Novel of Manners

The scene of the novel of manners ... draws on both the satiric touch-stone scene in which guilt is diffused and the satiro-sentimental scene of sexual threat and tears. Both the ironic observer of the Fielding novel and the Smollettian observer of delicate sensibility—one a controlling intelligence, the other a character—contribute to the heroine of the novel of manners. Those assistant satirists who surround the dumb man of feeling are as important as the spectra of different points of view in the Spectator Club and *Humphrey Clinker*. The essential elements, however, are the controlling and analytic intelligence of the Fielding novel and the Richardsonian concern with consciousness; but the latter, before it could influence the novel of manners, had to pass through satiric intermediaries.

It is possible to trace a line from the anti-romance of Cervantes, Sorel, and Furetière through the novels of Fielding, Smollett, and Burney to the novel of manners written by Jane Austen. The anti-romance contributes the basic structure for a study of manners not concerned exclusively with conduct book problems (what to do when two equally stringent rules apply at once) or with a reportorial description of different manners (the various "spy" and travel narratives). The basic situation simply involves the juxtaposition of two sets of values or manners (ideal-real, aristocratic-bourgeois, natural-unnatural, free-confined, individualist-conformist) and a protagonist who touches both. The protagonist is between the two areas; not completely committed to either, he is insecure, an unknown quantity seeking to

From *Satire and the Novel in Eighteenth-Century England*. ©1967 by Yale University. Yale University Press, 1967.

discover his true position in relation to them, or else he is solidly on the lower level but trying to pass himself off as the higher, or perhaps even trying to become the higher. The spectrum of possibility runs from the bastard or foundling who seeks self-identity to the fop who apes the externals of his betters.

The Richardsonian novel is a novel of manners in the sense that it is concerned with the relationship between the manners of the rising middle class and those of the declining aristocracy. If an analogy is possible between *Don Quixote* and *Pamela* or *Clarissa,* its usefulness lies in Richardson's employment of the romantically alluring image of the aristocratic rake to draw Pamela and Clarissa, with much talk of reforming him, to their respective fates. Richardson's aim is not criticism or analysis, however, but conflict, ending happily for Pamela, tragically for Clarissa. Neither heroine is presented primarily as aspiring to the aristocracy, but rather as pursued and persecuted by it. Clarissa in particular is ground to death between the wheels of the two classes. In both cases, Richardson expresses the feelings of the emergent bourgeoisie—a servant may marry her master, and a middle-class girl should be married, not raped, by an aristocrat (a view at variance with the Restoration comedy of manners); in short, the individual's integrity is paramount and depends on freedom of choice.

It was left for Fielding to turn from the dramatization of a conflict to an analysis of the relationship involved. Fielding, however, was not concerned with the relationship between the classes, but with the anti-romance subject of the relationship between the instincts of the individual and the code of manners that does not at every point fit them—either painfully distorting them or serving as a convenient mask for the hypocrite. Thus in *Joseph Andrews,* his anti-romance on *Pamela,* he opposes the real human behavior of Adams and Joseph to the middle-class manners of the Pamelas and Cibbers, which conceal or justify self-seeking. Quixotism is interpreted by Fielding as the ability to see through (or be unaffected by) the manners of one's society. In *Tom Jones* he uses the man motivated by natural feeling to criticize the conventions and customs of his society, including the aristocratic manners of the Bellasons and Fellamars. In a sense all of Fielding's work is constructed on the anti-romance situation; in his early works he shows the foppish imitators of fashion, which in this case is the false ideal of "greatness." But he treats Jones as Cervantes did Quixote, putting him and the Fellamars side by side, as feeling and form, and letting them comment on each other. To the extent that the virtues and vices of feeling and form are balanced—some virtue on both sides—*Tom Jones* becomes a novel of manners.

Fielding's novel also enormously broadens the scope of satiric irony in order to express a point of view that is judicious, understanding, and sympathetic and can encompass both form and feeling. However, it still leaves a broad gap between *Tom Jones* and *Pride and Prejudice*. One of the important breaks is the relationship between persuasion and dramatization, between reader and protagonist. Fielding's technical equipment permitted the reader's growing awareness, but it worked less well when he wished to dramatize the growing awareness of a character. In *Tom Jones* he attempted to make Tom's self-recognition correspond to the reader's. As early as book 8 Tom speaks out to correct the Old Man of the Hill, whose experience, like Tom's, has been colored by betrayal but whose generalization is that all men are evil. Tom has discovered, somewhere along the line, about the same time as the reader, that this is an oversimplification. He shows this even more strikingly with the puppet-master who, unwilling to acknowledge man's mixed nature, presents only paragons to instruct his audience. Jones tells him that he should have included Punch: "so far from improving, I think, by leaving him out and his merry wife Joan, you have spoiled your puppet-show" (bk. 12, chap. 5). When the puppet-master's wife discovers her maid making love with the Merry Andrew on the stage, the truth of Tom's view becomes apparent, and the gypsy episode confirms Tom's and the reader's realization that mercy is better than strict justice, that evil is in many cases a spot that darkens a character but does not destroy it. Tom later appears to see Black George's failure (stealing the £500) as an objectification of his own at Upton and elsewhere, when he pleads for him: "you must suffer me to call it weakness rather than ingratitude; for I am convinced the poor fellow loves me" (bk. 18, chap. 11).

One wonders, however, if the knowledge of mixed character is connected with Tom's more important disasters. It shows understanding in his relations with Black George and Molly but has no effect when applied as self-knowledge to his own case; indeed one goes from his talk with the Old Man to his escapade with Mrs. Waters, after which his views about mixed character sound like special pleading. The knowledge administered helps the reader but not Tom. It is the reader who needs to know about the complexity of actions in order to understand Tom; Tom only needs to learn prudence and to know himself. Therefore in terms of the main action of the novel—the need to complement Tom's feeling with form—the enlightened party remains the reader, and the character seems unaware of his problem. Knowledge that all people are fallible is hardly a help toward self-knowledge or self-discipline. The truth, I suspect, is that Fielding is still primarily interested in Tom as a corrective and as an example of character vs. conduct; he is not really interested in Tom's perception—the sine qua non of the novel of manners.

An ingénu cannot serve as the protagonist of a novel of manners. Joseph Andrews' innocence (and to a lesser degree Tom's) forces the reader to focus on the evil glaringly exposed, not on the hero's problems that may have caused him to become entangled with knaves. Joseph is never embarrassed: to be embarrassed one must see as well as be seen. Tom's embarrassment (for example, when he learns that Sophia knows of his behavior at Upton) points in a direction that Fielding never fully explores. Among the satirists, Smollett is responsible for this strain. The novel of manners protagonist and many secondary characters descend from the satiric observer as a character, whose gradual transformation we have followed from a public figure (whose motives and concerns are external and moral) to a private one (whose concerns are strictly internal and personal). Roderick Random acted as a satirist of society out of both desire for revenge (private) and moral conviction (public); by the time one reaches Captain Mirvan in *Evelina* personal considerations are the sole motive. However, only when an author can balance an interest in what happened per se with how it appeared to X, Y, and Z, can a novel like *Pride and Prejudice* be produced.

DR. PRIMROSE: THE IRONIC HERO

One of the missing links, the step beyond Fielding in the exploitation of irony as a fictional device, is supplied by Oliver Goldsmith's *The Vicar of Wakefield* (1766). This novel, so brilliant for at least half its length, is strangely underestimated, remaining a memory from childhood which, unlike *Gulliver* or *Crusoe,* cannot shake off the childish reading. There is perhaps no level the child has missed, and the pleasure of the adult is almost the same as that of the child. The *Vicar*'s great popularity and its influence on continental literature were due to Goldsmith's building his story on fairy-tale motifs and archetypal patterns that touched a sensitive chord in all readers and showed a way toward introducing romance into the realistic novel form. (Similar patterns in *Clarissa* were submerged under the close texture of observed experience—though they played their part in Richardson's popularity too.) As Smollett builds his novels around a structure of satiric exposition (with some romantic or sentimental plot elements), so Goldsmith builds his novel around the myths of the god who descends among humans as a traveler in search of hospitality, the ruler who passes among his people in disguise, and Jack and the Beanstalk. The most striking and central of the myths is the story of Job—his fortune lost, his house burnt down, both his daughters abducted, one (supposed) dead, his son about to be hanged, etc. The *Vicar* is a typical product of mixed genres, with many theatrical elements thrown in at the end.

In part, however, it is a close eighteenth-century precursor of *Pride and Prejudice,* and it still shows the scaffolding that has been shed or more thoroughly disguised by Austen. To begin, we must go back to a slightly earlier work. The first "Chinese Letters" were published early in 1760; they were reworked as much as possible and published as *The Citizen of the World* in May 1762. Goldsmith wrote the *Vicar* at this time or shortly after, although it was not published until 1766. In other words, Dr. Primrose follows chronologically hard on Lien Chi Altangi. Goldsmith's Chinese observer carries the associations of a country very unlike the Persia of Montesquieu's *Lettres Persanes,* with its seraglio, passion, and adventure; China recalls wisdom, tradition, conservatism, and the like. Unlike the noble savage (Voltaire's Huron), Lien Chi Altangi brings something more with him than simplicity; his comments are often sharpened by irony, particularly as he becomes accustomed to the new country and can analyze both it and China with some detachment, juxtaposing their different manners. But this is not to suggest that he is only an ironic observer. Often he sees the truth through a child's eyes or through the haze of conflicting conventions, and often at the beginning and occasionally at the end his divergent point of view exposes him to satire. In a memorable scene he is charmed by a young lady he meets on the street, from whom he generalizes about the kindness of English ladies; he never suspects that she is a prostitute until she fails to return the watch she has volunteered to have repaired for him. His true criticisms of the fantastic fashions of London women are followed by his adverse comments on their white teeth and unconstricted feet. He is, after all, Goldsmith points out, from a country with as many foolish customs of its own. The effect in general is of two sets of manners—some good, some bad—juxtaposed, rather than one set (bad) criticized by the other (good).

There is nothing new about this figure. The satirist tries to invent a central figure who can convey as much varied satire as possible. When Goldsmith came to write the *Vicar,* however, he must have begun with two ideas—to present a Parson Adams character and to have a Fieldingesque commentator as his supposed "author." The *Vicar,* it should be remembered, comes from the pen of an essayist; it represents Goldsmith's first step toward dramatic form. It is the first of the early novels to use an ironic narrator who is a central character of the action as well—both an ironist and the object of dramatic irony.

Dr. Primrose sees more than the people around him and lets the reader, and sometimes the people themselves, know about it. But the reader sees still more than Primrose does. In short, Goldsmith goes one step beyond Fielding, at the same time shedding some of the creaking machinery involved in the omniscient "historian" of Fielding's novels (but stopping far short of the irrational order of *Tristram Shandy*). He has made the irony part of his speaker's temperament, creating a more complex as well as a wittier person while at the same time adding a dramatic irony that was impossible in Fielding's kind of narrative. The situation is still basically a satiric one, focusing on the pretensions to gentility of Mrs. Primrose and her daughters. They are ridiculous; she is unpleasant. The family of a poor parson (he has come down in the world), they try to emulate the gentry with dress, carriage, even a family portrait, and they become prey to the aristocratic wolf who appears in the shape of Squire Thornhill.

Goldsmith duplicates the *Clarissa* situation of seduction, but he treats it in a different way from either Richardson or his satiric equivalent, Smollett. His focus is on the manners of the sheep rather than on the wolf, and it is not a sentimental focus; he studies their aspirations and the Quixotic effects in absurd behavior and in a blindness to the real situation in which a wolf is approaching ever nearer. This emphasis is achieved by placing at the center of the narrative the clever man, the ironist who though he sees through his wife and daughters yet bows to their wishes. He may surreptitiously throw away their face washes, but he allows himself to be guided by them in the posing of the family portrait, the dispatching of the good Burchell, and the encouraging of the evil Squire Thornhill. In fact, although he sees through his wife's values, he unconsciously shares some of them; his contempt of Burchell, the "man of broken fortune," emerges in his fear that his daughter Sophia may in fact fall in love with him:

> But I had too good an opinion of Sophia's understanding, and was too well convinced of her ambition, to be under any uneasiness from a man of broken fortune.

> Nor could I conceive how so sensible a girl as my youngest [Sophia], could thus prefer a man of broken fortune to one whose expectations were much greater.

To appreciate the originality of Goldsmith's conception one must look back on the *Vicar* from the vantage point of *Pride and Prejudice*. There the first-person protagonist has been replaced by a guiding intelligence resembling Fielding's ironic "historian," but the central character, Elizabeth Bennet, is an ironist like Dr. Primrose. While observing accurately the pretensions of those around her, she cannot see with complete clarity and is deceived by the manners of both Wickham and Darcy (as Primrose is by Squire Thornhill and Burchell). The theme that emerges from this kind of a central character, however elemental in Dr. Primrose, is self-knowledge and the growth to self-realization. When he recognizes his mistake about the two Thornhills, Dr. Primrose also recognizes something—however rudimentary the treatment as compared with Austen's—about himself.

Dr. Primrose is in the position later taken over by Elizabeth Bennet, and he is rather like her in his self-assurance, wit, and limited insight. But he is the head of a family, and his equivalent (if not direct descendant) is Mr. Bennet, a more intelligent version who like Primrose regards his hideous wife and foolish daughters with weary irony but is easygoing; Mr. Bennet has given up the fight and merely observes amusedly. As a result he offers a contrast to his daughter Elizabeth, whose limitation is not withdrawal. Mr. Bennet is ultimately responsible for the fate of Lydia and realizes it, just as Dr. Primrose shares responsibility for the fate of Olivia and at length recognizes his mistake. The whole Primrose family is, in fact, lifted bodily into *Pride and Prejudice:* the ignorant, pretentious, social-climbing mother, the duped Olivia, and the one sensible daughter, Sophia, have their equivalents in Mrs. Bennet, her daughters, and the two sensible sisters, Elizabeth and Jane. The two suitors in the *Vicar* are like Wickham and Darcy—one with surface charm who is actually a Lovelace seducer (Squire Thornhill), the other less prepossessing, in fact somewhat cynical and misanthropic (Burchell). (Burchell bears the same relation to Primrose as Drybone [the Man in Black] to Lien Chi Altangi, telling his life story, serving as a guide, and allowing him to see beyond appearances. But Primrose dismisses his guide, and this is the beginning of his troubles.) The main question and plot stimulus of the *Vicar*—and of all Austen novels—is how to marry off the daughters. The first thought Dr. Primrose has when he learns that he has lost his fortune is how he will make suitable marriages for his daughters, and this concern drives him (against his better nature) into his wife's camp in his opinion of Burchell. By putting the father in the center, Goldsmith makes marriage the important matter of the novel—but of course from the father's point of view; Austen puts one of the marriageable daughters in the center but gives her some of the detachment of the father in relation to the mating rite.

The first difference between the two novels, as I have noted, is in the protagonist's role. From Fanny Burney's *Evelina* Austen no doubt learned the usefulness and flexibility of the bright young girl's point of view. Her very youth makes the theme more convincingly one of growth and self-knowledge. At the same time, however, by keeping a narrator who more

clearly and unambiguously sees through Elizabeth—though is often parallel
to Elizabeth—Austen avoids immersing the reader in Elizabeth's emotions.
In this sense Goldsmith is braver than Austen, and like Swift he trusts to his
own ability to keep the proper distance between Primrose and the reader
without benefit of the omniscient narrator.

All that has been said about the *Vicar* applies only to the first seventeen
chapters. Goldsmith may have run out of ideas at that point, or he may have
picked up his real interest, the myth of Job. Suddenly he has Primrose
embark on a journey (talking predictably about life as a journey), and he
reverts to an older genre, the picaresque; he loses the wonderfully tight,
controlled, and effective microcosm of the family and slips back into the
world of the "Chinese Letters" with satiric essays on punishment, liberty,
and contemporary drama. While a great part of the originality of the first
part comes from its tightness of structure, Goldsmith now accepts Smollett's
permissive definition of a novel and gives digressions such as George's account of his life. The romantic and mythic elements emerge to full prominence. Goldsmith makes Primrose a true Job, relies on coincidences (the
meetings with Miss Wilmot, George, and Olivia), and builds the disguise
imagery that was subordinated to the plot in the first half into a pseudo-
unifying force. (Disguise is a common ground for the two conflicting aspects
of the *Vicar*. As a romance motif, it helps to define Burchell's role as the
disguised prince and the villainous abductors' role. As a device of the novel
of manners, however, disguise runs from the posing of the Primroses above
their proper class, to the whores who pose as Lady Blarney and Miss Carolina Wilelmina Amelia Skeggs, to Jenkinson who wears actual disguises as
part of his confidence racket.) The ballads and interpolated tales become
more frequent. As Frederick A. Hilles has pointed out [in his introduction to
the Everyman edition], these are necessary to make the narrative seem more
real by contrast and, with the preposterous reversals and recognitions of the
stories, to prepare the reader for the end. But the only blatant romance
occurrence in the first half is the fall of Primrose's youngest into a raging
stream, from which Burchell rescues her, and I am inclined to suspect that
this, as well as the ballad of *Edwin and Angelina,* are interpolations in the
light of the second half. The problem of the second half is not, however,
germane to my argument, which is only that in the first seventeen chapters
of the *Vicar* Goldsmith, starting with an anglicized Lien Chi Altangi, a
family setting, and the problem of marriage, produced a new and original
form which augmented the picaresque form of Fielding and contributed
another stage in the transition from satire to Austen's novel of manners.

R. F. BRISSENDEN

The Sentimentality
of The Vicar of Wakefield

The Reverend Dr. Primrose, Goldsmith's Vicar of Wakefield, is, like Parson Adams and Parson Yorick, a Christian hero. He "unites in himself," says the author in the advertisement to his tale, "the three greatest characters upon earth; he is a priest, an husbandman, and the father of a family." He is moreover the embodiment of some of the principal sentimental virtues. He is charitable, humane, optimistic and in general readier to think well rather than ill of his fellow men. All his family, he tells us, "had but one character, that of being all equally generous, credulous, simple, and inoffensive." Since his moral assessments of the situations in which he finds himself are spontaneous and unselfish, he could be described as a man of feeling, but feelings in his case are always grounded in a coherent set of Christian principles, and they are always vigorously implemented in positive action. He is a man of sentiment, of sense rather than sensibility; and his determination to govern his behaviour according to principle often gets him into comic trouble with the world. When his son George is about to marry Miss Arabella Wilmot, Primrose endangers the whole scheme by refusing to compromise his beliefs on the subject of monogamy which he discovers to be diametrically opposed to those held by Miss Wilmot's father. Principle again carries the day a short while later when, learning that he has suddenly lost his fortune, Primrose refuses to let the marriage proceed under false pretences.

The purpose of the action in the novel is to display the Vicar of Wakefield

From *Virtue in Distress: Studies in the Novel of Sentiment from Richardson to Sade.* © 1974 by R. F. Brissenden and R. L. Brissenden. Macmillan, 1974.

in a number of testing situations. "He is drawn," Goldsmith tells us, "as ready to teach, and ready to obey, as simple in affluence, and majestic in adversity." Like Job, he loses his fortune and practically loses his family. At the nadir of his adventures he is presented to us ill, injured, penniless and in prison. His house has been burned down, one of his daughters appears to have been ruined by the local nobleman, Squire Thornhill, and his eldest son George is also in prison, chained and under sentence of death for having sent a challenge to the man who has wronged his sister.

But Primrose never loses his faith nor his moral energy. He preaches to the other prisoners, and once he has got them to listen to him persuades them to spend their time in useful work—i.e, in making small articles which they can sell. "Thus in less than a fortnight I had formed them into something social and humane, and had . . . brought [them] from their native ferocity into friendship and obedience." At the same time he consoles his fellow sufferers with the promise that although the rich man may be happy on earth the poor and the wretched who believe in God will be rewarded with an eternity of bliss—a reward which they are much more likely to attain since poverty and imprisonment cut them off from so many dangerous temptations.

But Primrose's virtue is rewarded in a much more immediate and tangible manner. A good fairy arrives in the shape of the cheerful vagabond Mr Burchell, whom Primrose has befriended earlier on in the story. "Former benevolence [is] now repaid with unexpected interest," as the heading to chapter 12, volume 2 puts it. Mr Burchell turns out to be Sir William Thornhill in disguise, the philanthropic uncle of the wicked young Squire Thornhill. Sir William marries one of Primose's daughters, he provides a dowry for the other (who turns out to be genuinely married to his nephew), George's fetters are struck off, Primrose's fortunes are restored, and all's well that ends well. When Primrose, at the beginning of the novel, sends his son out into the world to seek his fortune he urges him to make the following text his consolation: *"I have been young, and now am old; yet never saw I the righteous man forsaken, or his seed begging their bread."* The happy dénouement would seem to be meant to demonstrate the validity of this hopeful statement.

But the whole process of the action of the story has been to negate it. The more virtuously Primrose and his family behave the more cruelly they are made to suffer at the hands of fortune and their fellow men. A synopsis of the plot up to, but not including, the happy reversal with which it is rounded off would make *The Vicar of Wakefield* sound like an episode in Sade's *Justine*—it seems to demonstrate not only that the practice of virtue is not rewarded in this world but also that it is likely to attract the most outrageously bad luck. The burning down of Primrose's house is like the final destruction and violation of Justine by a bolt of lightning—a gratuitous kick in the teeth delivered by the malevolent universe in which we have to live. The structure of *The Vicar of Wakefield,* regarded as a whole, is thus profoundly sentimental, in the modern sense of the term.

Its sentimentality for the most part, however, is not disturbing, and it is interesting to speculate as to why this should be so (the one distasteful element in the fortunate conclusion is the transformation of Squire Thornhill into a suitable husband for Olivia—he is a much nastier character in fact than Richardson's Mr B.). *The Vicar of Wakefield* remains a genuinely charming and delightful book. One of the main reasons for this is that the classically comic plot is so obviously artificial. It has the happy air of a deliberately contrived, almost magical ritual—a charm enacted against wicked men and evil days in which we are cordially invited to take part. Moreover Goldsmith's picture of life in the country is at once realistic and idyllic: the framework may be artificial, but the domestic rural world of the Primroses which it encompasses is rendered with remarkable fidelity, liveliness and good humour. The catastrophes which overtake the family are kept in perspective by the gentle comedy—Primrose slyly tipping the face-wash in the fire, or Mr Burchell, with his chorus of "Fudge!," undercutting the high-flown sophisticated chatter of the London whores. It is easy to understand how the young Goethe, embarked on his own idyllic holiday with the family at Sesenheim, could feel, as he tells us in *Dichtung und Wahrheit,* that he had walked into the Primrose household itself.

Nonetheless in the final assessment there is something worrying about the novel, a discordant note which all Goldsmith's charm cannot completely disguise. And the source of the discord can be located not so much in the Vicar of Wakefield himself as in his guardian angel, the man who saves him and his family from destruction, Mr Burchell, or Sir William Thornhill in disguise. Sir William Thornhill, as he presents himself through the mask of Burchell to the Primroses, is a melancholy man of feeling. The conversation between him and the Vicar is of unusual interest, and deserves to be quoted at length:

> "What!" cried I, "is my young landlord then the nephew of
> a man whose virtues, generosity, and singularities are so univer-
> sally known? I have heard of Sir William Thornhill represented
> as one of the most generous, yet whimsical, men in the kingdom;

a man of consummate benevolence"—"Something, perhaps, too
much so," replied Mr. Burchell, "at least he carried benevolence
to an excess when young; for his passions were then strong, and
as they were all upon the side of virtue, they led it up to a
romantic extreme. . . . He loved all mankind; for fortune prevented him from knowing that there were rascals. Physicians tell
us of a disorder in which the whole body is so exquisitely sensible, that the slightest touch gives pain: what some have thus
suffered in their persons, this gentleman felt in his mind. The
slightest distress, whether real or fictitious, touched him to the
quick, and his soul laboured under a sickly sensibility of the
miseries of others. Thus disposed to relieve, it will be easily
conjectured, he found numbers disposed to solicit; his profusions
began to impair his fortune, but not his good-nature; that, indeed, was seen to encrease as the other seemed to decay: he grew
improvident as he grew poor; and though he talked like a man
of sense, his actions were those of a fool."

In short he began to dissipate his fortune, and also to lose confidence in his
ability to assess the characters and motives of his fellow men. In order to
repair the damage both to himself and his finances "he travelled through
Europe on foot." This left him (for some inexplicable reason) "more af-
fluent than ever." And now, therefore, "his bounties are more rational and
moderate than before; but still he preserves the character of an humourist,
and finds most pleasure in eccentric virtues." Since Sir William Thornhill is
so important in the moral scheme of Goldsmith's fable it is interesting to
note the terms in which he describes himself. He has a "sickly sensibility,"
he has behaved more like a fool than a man of sense, "he preserves the
character of an humourist," i.e., an oddity, and he "finds most pleasure in
eccentric virtues." "Eccentric" is perhaps the key word: Thornhill is able to
preserve his integrity and also to operate effectively if erratically as a moral
agent only by functioning *outside* the society to which he belongs. He does
not live on his estates, he moves amongst his tenants in disguise, he is utterly
incapable *because of his exquisite sensibility* of playing a normal part in the
community. Yet he represents in their most highly developed form the moral
ideals of this society from which he is in a sense excluded. Primrose, the
"normal" man, occupies a central place in this same society—husbandman,
priest, and father—but it destroys him. Burchell / Thornhill is thus not
merely a Harounel-Rashid figure, the romantic "someone in disguise" who
turns up in the nick of time to set things right. He is a symbol of alienation,

the dispossessed conscience of a sick society. And although like George Primrose (and presumably like Goldsmith in his happier moments) he recalls his travels on the Continent cheerfully enough, his motive for undertaking them was despair. Against the carefree image of the happy wanderer playing his flute to the simple peasants one should set the opening lines of *The Traveller,* which Goldsmith published in 1765 (a year before the appearance of *The Vicar of Wakefield*) and which bears the subtitle, *A Prospect of Society:*

> Remote, unfriended, melancholy, slow,
> Or by the lazy Scheld, or wandering Po;
> Or onward, where the rude Carinthian boor
> Against the houseless stranger shuts the door;
> Or where Campania's plain forsaken lies,
> A weary waste expanded to the skies,
> Where'er I roam, whatever realms to see,
> My heart untravell'd fondly turns to thee;
> Still to my brother turns, with ceaseless pain,
> And drags at each remove a lengthening chain.

The implications of *The Vicar of Wakefield,* ostensibly a sentimental comedy, are thus at bottom as pessimistic and as elegiac as those of *The Deserted Village* and *The Traveller.* One feels that for Goldsmith society appears to be so irrational, so cruel, and so economically inefficient and inequitable, that it is extremely difficult if not impossible for the ordinary, well-intentioned, morally responsible man to live the good life. For Dr Primrose to survive he needs the magical assistance of Sir William Thornhill. It could be said that Tom Jones similarly needs the magical assistance of Squire Allworthy—but he does not need it nearly so desperately. Allworthy in the end merely represents the good luck which Tom in a sense deserves: it is easy to believe that he would have had more than a fighting chance of winning through somehow on his own resources. But one cannot feel this about the Primrose family. The structure of *The Vicar of Wakefield,* and in particular the division of moral responsibility between the Vicar himself and Sir William Thornhill, reflects a radical disquiet with the nature of man and society, a disquiet which forces Goldsmith into sentimentality.

WAYNE C. BOOTH

"The Self-Portraiture of Genius":
The Citizen of the World
and Critical Method

"Dr. Goldsmith is one of the first men we now have as an author."
—SAMUEL JOHNSON, 1763

No one who read the "Chinese Letters" of Goldsmith as they first appeared in 1760–61 could have overlooked their great range in subject and
effect. Commissioned as "papers of amusing character," they exhibited
what every reader would expect in periodical letters: a variety of instruction
and delight confessedly miscellaneous. And they were uniformly judged, so
far as we can tell, by such traditional rhetorical standards as pleasure and
utility (for the reader) and variety, good sense, and genius (in the author):

> Were we to examine these reflections of *our Citizen of the World*
> by the standard of originality, our pleasure would be greatly
> diminished; but let us view them with regard to utility, and we
> must confess their merit. What seems cloying to an hundred
> persons of fastidious appetites, may prove wholesome delicious
> nourishment to thousands. These letters, if we mistake not, made
> their first appearance in a daily news-paper, and were necessarily
> calculated to the meridian of the multitude. . . . It is rather ex-
> traordinary, that the philosophic *Lien Chi Altangi* could handle
> so many topics agreeably, and sustain the fatigue of so long a
> course without weariness, than that he has sometimes stumbled.

From *Modern Philology* 73, no. 4 (May 1976). © 1976 by the University of
Chicago.

> All his observations are marked with good sense, genius fre-
> quently breaks the fetters of restraint, and humour is sometimes
> successfully employed to enforce the dictates of reason.
>
> (*Critical Review,* 1762)

Such commodious rhetorical standards were almost automatic in criticism of the time, especially when it dealt with commodious forms like the
periodical essay. And for nearly two centuries critics took them for granted
in judging *The Citizen*—just as anyone today would take them for granted
in giving a commonsense explanation of why "The Talk of the Town," say,
is superior to the personal essays in this week's student newspaper. It would
never have occurred to John Forster, for example, writing in 1848, to worry
about whether the collected letters made a unified, or coherent, or organic
whole. For him, the test was still rhetorical: *The Citizen* "amused the hour,
was wise for the interval beyond it, is still diverting and instructing us, and
will delight generations yet unborn."

To us it may seem evident that when the series of "Chinese Letters"
was edited into a book, *The Citizen of the World,* the author invited a
different, more "organic" standard. The miscellaneity that may be appropriate in a periodical, visible proof of the author's genius, can easily become
a major problem for any critic who takes the implied claim of the "editor"
seriously: "Here is a *book.*" Has he made a book or has he not? Curiously
enough, nobody seems to have asked that question seriously until our own
time.

In the twentieth century we do not readily praise an author simply for
keeping us awake and engaged with variety. At least until quite recently,
serious critics have preferred questions about the unity of the work to
questions about the author's genius and powers of communication and the
audience's pleasure or profit. The same "variety" that had delighted rhetorical critics becomes, for a critic seeking the unity of made objects, a
problem to be explained, or even a self-evident fault.

It is not my intention in what follows to argue that to seek organic
unities in such a work is wrong. I shall try to show only that much of
Goldsmith's art is obscured by any predetermined quest for "intrinsic"
harmonies. Though the rhetorical critics of Goldsmith's time disappoint us
by their generality, never accounting fully for the genius and variety they
praise, their interest in such qualities can remind us that there is after all a
genuine "art of the miscellaneous." And it is an art that I think no modern
criticism has fully honored.

I

Suppose we begin, in looking for the art of *The Citizen,* not determined to find any particular known artistic form or established kind of unity, but simply looking for signs of skill. To do so relieves us at once of all anxiety about whether the work "as a whole" is unified. It does not, of course, free us from an interest in form, because we could never discern any skill that was not in some sense an exhibition of form. But in turning to Goldsmith's skill we can at least for a time attend *to whatever binds his readers to him,* without worrying about how the various bonds relate to each other. I shall begin with the more obviously "formal" or "intrinsic" skills and move toward the more obviously rhetorical or "extrinsic," but—as even my first example will show—these cannot in Goldsmith be finally distinguished.

Perhaps Goldsmith's most obvious skill is the one least neglected, the beauty of each period. What *is* the excellence of a sentence like this? "The ignorant critic and dull remarker can readily spy blemishes in eloquence or morals, whose sentiments are not sufficiently elevated to observe a beauty; but such are judges neither of books nor of life." The delicate parallelism of

| critic | eloquence | books |
| remarker | morals | life |

is easy to note but difficult indeed to explain. And what new quality is added when, to such a seemingly completed form, Goldsmith adds the following? "They can diminish no solid reputation by their censure, nor bestow a lasting character by their applause: In short, I found by my search, that such only can confer real fame upon others, who have merit themselves to deserve it." Traditionally our talk about neoclassical style has been general in the extreme—a few commonplaces about "periodic" and "loose" sentence structure, a few untested and dogmatic utterances about correctness and decorum. Surely a serious criticism could be much more precise in accounting for such structures, as remarkable in their way as the most carefully formed lyric poems. I cannot pretend to say what a full analysis of style in *The Citizen* would reveal, in the hands of someone alert to linguistic and stylistic subleties. But it would surely show a multiplicity of forms each qualifying as art in anyone's definition. Like Goldsmith's paragraphs, and indeed his individual essays viewed separately, these brief forms are in themselves complete, self-fulfilling, autonomous, inviting to pure contemplation, even while amusing or edifying. The beginnings "require" their middles and ends at least as surely as can be said of the parts of any poem or play. And the structures can be said to complete themselves internally; expunge or transpose any part and you destroy the whole.

Similarly, I have found no detailed analysis of how short essays are organized by Goldsmith or other great essayists. What are the specific formal beauties of a 1,000-word Tatler, Spectator, Idler, Rambler, or Bee? How do patterns of climax, anticlimax, refrain, imitation and transformation of traditional tropes and figures—how do these contribute to discernible excellence in the structure of particular essays? Has anyone looked at what happens when the criteria of transposability and expungability, invaluable in any genuine organicist criticism, are applied not to linear sequences of event and subject but to formal "musical" designs like these? What do we know about—not *poetic closure,* or *completion of intellectual arguments,* the signals of one kind of formal excellence in poems and philosophical works—but essayistic closure? Like all great periodical essayists, Goldsmith builds thousands of masterful short forms, yet criticism has for the most part, even in its encomiums, made him sound like a dabbler—or rather, it has given us no way to distinguish his kind of skill from dabbling.

Second, our "criticism of skills" must pursue the great variety of "superficial" thematic and dramatic sequences that Goldsmith plays with along his way. The most obvious of these is the relatively prolonged story of the adventures of Altangi's son culminating in his marriage to the beautiful slave, revealed, in what is clearly a parody of romantic endings, as the daughter of the Man in Black. But there are sequences as short as the two-letter adventure of Altangi with the London prostitute. In letter 8 he describes her as "one of those generous creatures," full of virtue, sincerity and truth, symbolizing a "land of innocence, and a people of humanity." In letter 9, published three days later, he has discovered the formal completion of this adventure: as the reader has known all along, enjoying a clear bit of dramatic irony, she proves to be one of the "infamous disciples of Han." The two letters thus make a self-contained unit, in one sense, but they also build connections with other moments, before and after, when Altangi will make a fool of himself.

II

Though there are literally thousands of sequences of these and other kinds, the further one pushes for "intrinsic" sequences, the more obvious it is that Goldsmith's own achievement is being touched only at a tangent. It seems likely that even the most penetrating search for "linear" or organic forms will leave us asking: But what of the *rest* of "the book"? Great patches of almost every letter, and a great number of letters, will not even have been mentioned, so long as we persist in talking of intrinsic interrelations, self-completed "within" the work. What, for example, of the ethical appeals in the sentence I have quoted, the character of author and reader implied in that talk about critical merit? And what about the many letters which are dictated by current events, discussed once or twice and then forgotten?—the war with France, the philanthropic "subscription in favour of the French prisoners," the publication of *Tristram Shandy*, the death of the king, the coronation, and so on.

An alert pursuer of intrinsic form might answer that once Altangi has commented upon any two such events, formal connections will have been established between them as a kind, and thus among all possible occasions. But it feels artificial indeed to describe them in any language of intrinsic form. We need instead rhetorical words like appetite, in the audience, and genius, or wisdom, or shrewdness, in the author. The most obvious appeal of such occasional pieces is to particular readers who are preheated for the piece by their interest in the event itself. Intrinsic terms cannot do justice either to the *desire* that readers would feel to see what, this week, the citizen will have to say about event X; or the *pleasure* they would take in the account; or the *appetite* they will then feel for some unspecified commentary on some as yet unknown future public event; or their *admiration* for the skillful author who promises more of the same. Goldsmith clearly had his attention as much on his audience and their experience as on any effort to complete one more beautifully articulated structure. And insofar as we wish to appreciate his skill, we must somehow reconstruct ourselves as his kind of audience. We shall thus almost certainly require some assistance from historical inquiry—the work, *in this view of its artistic excellence*—is *not* self-subsistent.

We might, of course, deplore such moments as lapses, as excrescences on the body of his art; we might choose to ignore them or to recognize them only as nonart, just *because* rhetorical considerations have led to a neglect of coherence. The temptation to do so will be greater if we accept the modern commonplace that correlates excellence strictly with universality or permanence of appeal. Insofar as Goldsmith deliberately caters to a "temporary" interest in his audience, so the doctrine runs, he repudiates *art*— and of course he risks losing the interest of any serious critic in a later time. *We* have no immediate interest in whether the nobility in 1760 were "degenerate," or in whether the French in 1760 were less disinterested in their philanthropy than the English, or in whether "our" funeral elegies written upon the "great" were ridiculous. Only insofar as Goldsmith has been able

to relate such parochial interests to some universal concern can I allow him
to have made art out of occasional materials.

This is not the place to deal fully with the issues of evaluation raised by
such a doctrine. But we can perhaps question it to the extent of recognizing
that many of the most interesting questions about Goldsmith's art, including that question of most concern to us—what *is* his art?—will be ruled out
or obscured if we take the doctrine at face value.

The classical unities presupposed that the creating of beautiful design
and its recognition by a reader or spectator was the primary aesthetic bond
between maker and receiver. The rules of unity were thus still "rhetorically"
expressed, in contrast with any criticism that cares most for how parts relate
organically to wholes. In deciding that even the classical rules could be
ignored for superior rhetorical purposes, critics like Pope and Johnson were
thus making no difficult decision, since they had seen those rules in rhetorical terms from the beginning. In our time, however, those of us who have
tried—and I have often myself tried hard—to describe "objective" qualities
and forms, putting effects on audiences to one side, ask ourselves to give up
much more of our critical baggage when we abandon a search for unity,
coherence, or integrity of design and look for what might be called structures of appeal.

III

One might attempt to list the appeals in the order in which they are
experienced, *if* they were in fact met as discrete appeals. But it is in the
nature of "variety" that a given stroke will carry more than one appeal.
Consider the opening paragraph of the "Editor's Preface":

> The schoolmen had formerly a very exact way of computing the
> abilities of their Saints or authors. Escobar, for instance, was
> said to have learning as five, genius as four, and gravity as seven.
> Caramuel was greater than he. His learning was as eight, his
> genius as six, and his gravity as thirteen. Were I to estimate the
> merits of our Chinese Philosopher by the same scale, I would not
> hesitate to state his genius still higher; but as to his learning and
> gravity, these I think might safely be marked as nine hundred
> and ninety nine, within one degree of absolute frigidity.

Here we meet at least three major appeals described below, in addition to
the formal skills described in part 1: (1) appeals to the reader's self-esteem
(we are superior to those pedantic schoolmen); (2) satire (again the

schoolmen); (3) pleasure in irony (we learn at once that the pairing of Saints and authors and the phrase "very exact" in the first sentence, like the word "greater" in the second, cannot be taken at face value; greater means smaller, or at least more solemn; genius means frigidity; high marks mean low marks; and so on).

It is, of course, impossible to separate these three sharply from each other or from the formal appeals I have described. Nevertheless, if we are to see just how much was being said when traditional critics praised Goldsmith's variety, we must risk analysis:

1. *Appeals to the reader's self-esteem (what must be called flattery if and when Goldsmith does not believe that the ascription of virtue is justified).* As citizen of London, I pick up the *Public Ledger* and I find myself congratulated for being: (*a*) An Englishman—that is, citizen of a nation that on the whole is the most generous, most enlightened, most advanced, best governed, in a word the most "polite" of all (e.g., letter 4); (*b*) A cosmopolitan—that is, like the author I am a citizen of the world. Though patriotic, I am too sophisticated to talk without irony of my patriotism, and I really take all mankind into my tolerant, amused vision; (*c*) A penetrating critic of the folly and greed that surround me, *even* here in England: I am the kind of person who can savor both the cosmic misreadings committed by Lien Chi Altangi and the comedy of British idiosyncrasy viewed in a universal light (e.g., letter 45).

2. *Pleasure in satire.* Merely to list the satiric objects—most of them reinforcing the first appeal—would fill pages: many different kinds and manifestations of pride, luxury, license, hypocrisy, superstition, ambition, pedantry, and fraudulence; varieties of ignorance and folly, in politics, in marriage customs, in scholarship and the arts, in travel, medicine, religion; many specific "humors," like the spleen and other kinds of hypochondria, social climbing, pretensions to wisdom; a variety of "classes" attacked in whole or part, such as women who aspire to masculine achievement, noblemen who dabble in the arts; and so on.

The objects as a list only hint at what any one satiric letter shows clearly: the satire is for the most part amiable, the reader for the most part cheerfully exempted from its charge. He can read safely as attacks are made on people of other nations, other classes, other professions. Even if he happens to be a doctor, say, the caricature of a quack will probably not cut too close to the bone. Yet it comes close enough to give the reader the *illusion* that he is broad-minded in tolerating it. Rarely does Goldsmith allow a depth that might seriously disturb an attentive reader, and even then, as in the City Night-Piece (letter 117), the literary mode in which the potentially shattering questions are raised is so conventional that the reader can easily maintain his distance: it is Altangi, the foreign visitor, who cries, "Why, why was I born a man, and yet see the sufferings of wretches I cannot relieve." The attack on the evils of poverty, and the threat of an attack on wealth, is finally deflected to another question entirely: "Why was this heart of mine formed with so much sensibility! or why was not my fortune adapted to its impulse! Tenderness, without a capacity of relieving, only makes the man who feels it more wretched than the object which sues for assistance." Which leaves *us* with an easy escape hatch.

One might, with a little intellectual stretching and considerable cynicism, incorporate all of the remaining appeals under these first two. But Goldsmith quite obviously did not believe, nor did he expect his readers to believe, that every human motive fell either under the enhancement of self or the degradation of others. In talking of *The Citizen* it is important not to attempt abstract classification along logically coherent lines. The pleasure of learning something, for example, or the pleasure of detecting an irony, have both, by some philosophers, been reduced to nothing more than the pleasure of being flattered. Here I shall continue to assume what Goldsmith would assume: that there are many kinds of human motivation, with degrees of authenticity, disinterestedness, egoism, and fraudulence discernible in each kind.

3. *Pleasure in recollection of commonplace wisdom.* As early reviewers noted, the level of instruction here is never threateningly high. Whether the instruction comes from behind an ironic surface, as in the story of the three lovers of British liberty (letter 4), or is offered directly, as in the "cautions on life, taken from a modern philosopher of China" (letter 83), we never go very deep, and we seldom are asked to think in unfamiliar ways. Readers who desire depth can go read Hume. Readers who want to be instructed delightfully, even comfortably, can read sound moral thought like this: "Avoid such performances where vice assumes the face of virtue, seek wisdom and knowledge without ever thinking you have found them. A man is wise, while he continues in the pursuit of wisdom; but when he once fancies that he has found the object of his enquiry, he then becomes a fool. Learn to pursue virtue from the man that is blind, who never makes a step without first examining the ground with his staff."

Anyone who is tempted to scoff at this kind of reinforcement of truisms should think first of the modern examples he has himself enjoyed. Popular rhetoric in serial form, whether it gets collected or not, almost always includes a large element of such reiteration of established wisdom. In our own time more serialists who have succeeded have, it is true, dressed their received truths in the guise of daring, lonely originality: the *unpopular* and *skeptical* essays and radio addresses of Bertrand Russell, the many "slashing," "daring," "revolutionary," and "shocking" columnists whose collected pieces earn a following: the Jimmy Breslins, Murray Kemptons, Mike Roykos, and Hunter Thompsons, all claiming to forge new and unpopular truths. But we also have had many Westbrook Peglers, Max Raffertys, and William Buckleys, "daring" to revive old and equally conventional ones.

4. *Pleasure in new truth.* In Goldsmith, as in most popular essayists, we do find a smattering of what to many readers will seem daring novelty. He thus presents a curious mixture of "neoclassical" and "romantic"—that is, he will do so to anyone who divides the world into two parts, classical and romantic. Anyone reading through *The Citizen* in search of romantic tags will find them everywhere, and it would be easy to explain why Goldsmith, as a preromantic, did not really come into his own until the romantic period: only one London edition in his lifetime, only five London editions before 1790, and then *seven* editions between 1790 and 1800! Do we not here see the triumph of Goldsmith's (occasional) insistence on individuality and originality; of his questioning of universal standards of truth and beauty (he can sometimes sound almost like a modern anthropologist); of his radical skepticism about miracles and wonders; of his insistence on the value of novelty and change? (Almost a century later, Forster could see Goldsmith's radical ideas as a chief mark of his greatness. He offers several pages listing the occasions when "the Chinese citizen so lifted his voice that only in a later generation could he find his audience.)

But even though some of *The Citizen's* views would have seemed shocking to some readers in 1760, it is clear that Goldsmith works to transform the shocks into the endurable thrills of the mildly daring.

5. *Pleasure in ironic deciphering.* Though it is misleading to say that the whole of *The Citizen* is ironic, every commentator has been aware that much of it is. Most critics have recognized that part of our sense of Goldsmith's "variety" derives precisely from the almost impossibly quick shifts of tone he expects of us. Goldsmith knew many satires in which an exotic traveler observes local vices and foibles. But he capitalized more fully than any I have read on the possibilities for variety of effect that such a traveler can offer. Earlier "visitors" tend to stress one of three possibilities: (1) Steady satire on ridiculous local customs, as in the many versions of "The Devil on Crutches." (It is true that such satire is "steady" only in effect, not in tone. The narrator is seldom a "consistent" character; instead he is shifted at will from reliable to ironic statement, and back again, while the steady attack is maintained.) (2) Steady exploitation of interest in the exo-

tic—the traveler reveals how strange is the world he comes from. (3) Steady exploitation of the comic ignorance of the visitor, with irony in every line.

Goldsmith's choice was to create an extraordinarily rich mixture of all three, and we should not be surprised that his diversity has produced confusion and controversy, not just in our own time, when ironologists abound and invite angry denunciations for overinterpretation, but from the very beginning. Readers early were troubled because Lien Chi Altangi was not consistently the exotic visitor, wise in *Chinese* matters, ignorant of *English* ways. In his wonderfully complex "Editor's Preface" Goldsmith says that many readers at first "were angry not to find him [the Citizen] as ignorant as a Tripoline ambassador, or an Envoy from Jujac." But instead of a straightforward defense of his Citizen, Goldsmith provides a shifting, playful mixture of bona fides and undercuttings:

> The distinctions of polite nations are few; but such as are peculiar to the Chinese, appear in every page of the following correspondence. The metaphors and allusions are all drawn from the East. Their formality our author carefully preserves. Many of their favourite tenets in morals are illustrated. The Chinese are always concise, so is he. Simple, so is he. The Chinese are grave and sententious, so is he. But in one particular, the resemblance is peculiarly striking: the Chinese are often dull; and so is he. Nor has my assistance been wanting. . . . In the intimacy between my author and me, he has usually given me a lift of his Eastern sublimity, and I have sometimes given him a return of my colloquial ease.

And then, in a manner close to the self-conscious narration of the *Tristam Shandy* that the Citizen is to attack in letter 53, the editor interrupts a fit of moralizing about the taste of the times: "During this fit of morality, lest my reader should sleep, I'll take a nap myself, and when I awake tell him my dream." The dream suggests the variety that is to come: it mocks those who have offered "the furniture, frippery and fireworks of China" and portrays Goldsmith as offering "a small cargoe of Chinese morality." But then it mocks that decision, sending his "wheelbarrow" full of offerings to the bottom of the Thames. Waking in a fright, the editor then turns to discuss himself. Neither a poet nor a philosopher, "at present I belong to no particular class. I resemble one of those solitary animals, that has been forced from its forest to gratify human curiosity. My earliest wish was to escape unheeded through life; but I have been set up for half-pence, to fret and scamper at the end of my chain. Tho' none are injured by my rage, I am naturally too savage to court any friends by fawning. Too obstinate to be taught new tricks; and too improvident to mind what may happen, I am appeased, though not contented. Too indolent for intrigue, and too timid to push for favour, I am—But what signifies what am I."

Now this is a curious piling up of ironies indeed. The final question must surely be answered: "Your *book* signifies precisely what you are—but what you are can thus never be precisely identified with any *part* of your book. Even to say that you are 'ironic' or 'cosmopolitan' will oversimplify."

The word "irony" can obscure more than it illuminates. Even if we confine our interest to intended, stable, covert ironies considering only statements that Goldsmith requires us to reconstruct into meanings that he foreordains, we find at least three kinds, all of them more precise than the general, asserted ironic view that Professor Quintana and others have seen as the unifying principle of the book.

a) Goldsmith and the reader stand securely together as Altangi commits an error either of fact or judgment or both. "The [public] houses borrow very few ornaments from architecture; their chief decoration seems to be a paltry piece of painting, hung out at their doors or windows, at once a proof of their indigence and vanity."

b) Goldsmith, the reader, and Altangi stand securely together against some other victim: "You are not insensible, most reverend Fum Hoam, what numberless trades, even among the Chinese, subsist by the harmless pride of each other. Your nose-borers, feet-swathers, tooth-stainers, eyebrow pluckers, would all want bread, should their neighbours want vanity. These vanities, however, employ much fewer hands in China than in England; and a fine gentleman, or a fine lady, here dressed up to the fashion, seems scarcely to have a single limb that does not suffer some distortions from art." The effect is like that under *a*, except that here the narrative voice is not repudiated. What is complex beyond the reach of final explanation is the ordinary reader's successful operation in determining when Altangi's words must be reconstructed and when they must not be.

c) Goldsmith, Altangi, and the reader attend to some third narrative voice whose words they all understand either to be self-betrayals or unreliable commentary. The structure of the bond here is just like the others, but the surface effect is of further variety. The introduction of Beau Tibbs, for example, in letters 54 and 55, provides innumerable instances of shifts of tone, ranging from Tibb's giving himself away without anyone's noting it except in silent communion, to the overt judgment by Altangi that the "company of fools may at first make us smile, but at last never fails of rendering us melancholy." If I ask whether Goldsmith stands by that final generalization—whether, like many of Altangi's judgments, it is silently repudiated by Goldsmith—I discover just how remarkably controlled the tone is. No one, not even Professor Hopkins, has suggested that Altangi's condemnation is too harsh, or that Goldsmith is really attacking *him* on behalf of the misjudged Beau. Altangi is here so little our concern, in himself, that his generalizations do not even serve to characterize him further: they are "Goldsmith's" generalizations. Yet they are tonally quite unlike the many nonironic essays.

6. *Pleasure in the exotic.* Though this appeal overlaps the pleasure of learning, it includes a kind of titillation that has little to do with satisfying curiosity or feeding an appetite for wisdom. *The Citizen* ridicules those who succumb to fads and fashions. But at the same time, as Goldsmith knew it would, the book profits from its exotic aura. Chinese names, manners, maxims, and anecdotes sprinkle almost every letter, and when Goldsmith cannot find what he needs in his sources he freely turns Western legends and anecdotes into "ancient Chinese lore." We can be sure that even his most sophisticated readers, perforce moved by their reading into "the meridian" of pleased response, would enjoy the genuine exotica, while at the same time playing two other games he invites them to: recognizing and admiring some of his Western transformations, and guessing about doubtful cases.

7. *Pleasure in parody, particularly of the exotic.* Related both to the satire and to the other kinds of ironic invitation to reconstruct meanings, this appeal depends on readers' ability to recognize the clichés of exotic romance and to enjoy seeing them mocked. Like all forms of invitation to make use of information not given on the surface of a text, parody both flatters the reader (no. 1), satirizes (no. 2), and gives at least the illusion of conveying truth (nos. 3 and 4)—if only truth about the vulnerability of the original. It also requires the deciphering energy of irony (no. 5). Thus parody cannot be grasped without its producing some degree of identification with the author, since he has as much as asserted that the reader shares his knowledge and his evaluation of the original.

8. *Pleasure in comic drama.* Every critic, at least until recently, has mentioned that *The Citizen* contains a collection of notable characters, all comic or humorous. Some have noted that these characters are not only "humorous" but "humours," highly caricatured "two-dimensional" folk who go through the same paces each time they come on stage. The London characters, like those who engage in the oriental adventure and then come together in the final parodic wedding, are never offered as developed persons. It is in the nature of this genre that it will not permit a developed drama any more than it will permit a really serious development of philoso-

phy, a sustained and challenging comment or satire, a deep analysis of the psychology of Londoners or of their social structure, a developed literary criticism, or indeed any other kind of discourse that requires scope for its perfecting.

Altangi himself, one might object, is given sustained and elaborate portrayal. Hopkins argues that he is consistently undermined by irony and is thus a sustained center of dramatic interest. But the fact is that we seldom see him as a character in his own right: our attention is almost always on the "Goldsmith" for whose consistent rich maneuvers the inconsistent Altangi serves, sometimes as mask and sometimes as direct spokesman.

These eight do not exhaust the skills of this author and the pleasure and instruction they yield. We have not talked of his rich metaphoric gift, or of his ability to describe the London setting with great vividness, or of his mastery of the vocabulary of praise (letter 43), or of . . . .

IV

The only explicit portrait of the implied author who provides our center is that which Goldsmith himself gives in the preface. When interpreted through its intricate ironies, the identification with the captive bear or monkey is perhaps our best clue to the *kind* of thing Goldsmith knows himself to be attempting. I "belong to no particular class"—*except* of course the class of those solitary entertainers who fret and scamper to satisfy human curiosity. We find in his description (see above), as we find in the book, an author who is determined to entertain but who will do so with metaphors that bite and instruct through biting; a man determined to be more honest than most commentators; a man savage, obstinate, improvident, not contented; a shrewd, disillusioned man, but still benevolent; a cosmopolitan, sometimes indeed almost cynical about his spectators—yet he *will* entertain.

It follows that to list the implied virtues of intellect, morality, and imagination exhibited by the "author" does as little justice to him as any summary of any book does to the whole; paraphrase can violate the "structure" of our relation to an authorial character just as it can the life of a plot. The portrait is made up of *all* the appeals we have mentioned, themselves still an abstraction from the cumulative delight and instruction found in every line of every page.

Each virtue binds us further to "Goldsmith" each time it is exemplified. And each new exemplification reinforces our conviction about the chief virtue of all: imaginative richness. Thus we read on, or around and about, not to discover *what will happen* but to discover *what our hero's genius will reveal* when he turns to the next subject, and the next after that. There will of course be specific kinds of "suspense," yielding a sequential appeal, especially for contemporary readers; once Altangi has enlivened any current event with his wry eccentric vision, readers will expect and desire more of the same whenever another major event occurs. A letter on "a noble death" predicts a letter on the coronation; on such occasions, readers must have awaited Altangi's words with an engagement as intense, of its kind, as they would feel between acts 4 and 5 of a well-plotted play. But the nature of the engagement, though certainly *formed* in one sense, is largely obscured when one attempts to use the formal language that I touched on in part 1.

And usually the "suspense" will be even more generalized. Even after weeks and months of variety, even when readers might have begun to suspect that all subjects suitable to the genre have been exhausted, they will hunger for more—but more of what? Why, of "Goldsmith," regardless of his subject. The appetite has become so generalized, in a work like *The Citizen,* that it applies beyond the boundaries of the work; having consumed these 123 banquets, I shall of course go on to those offered in *The Bee.* Nor will it matter very much if some of them fall short of perfection. Once a strong literary character like that of "Goldsmith" has been established, even his way of being dull is interesting: it adds to our knowledge of his total character. Like any other addiction, this one will be adequately served even when the particular dose is of inferior grade. It is of course especially unimportant if, reading in 1976, I find passages that are dull unless viewed as historically revealing. It is true that this genre is especially vulnerable to time—depending on later readers' learning. But the important question of how local and universal appeals are related is too large for treatment here.

What is important is to recognize that our experience of this character—possessing as he does every admirable quality except those inimical to his genre (philosophical profundity, psychological depth, sustained *poetic* invention, etc.)—is as "tightly organized" in its way as is our experience of sequential forms. If we try to add or subtract virtues from his portrait, we begin to encounter criteria as rigorous as those we find in linear works when we try to expunge or transpose events or episodes or characters. Suppose we try to erase his benevolence, or his awareness of how awful and ridiculous men and women tend to be, or his wit, or his capacity for irony, or his determination to see British manners in a cosmopolitan light, or his anger about injustice and the cruelty of some British institutions, or his amused tolerance of harmless vices, or his beautifully sustained stylistic grace and "correctness." Any of these virtues lost would weaken our engagement. What is more, it is hard to think of others that could be added. To imagine other virtues and ways of realizing them in serial essays would require of me comparable "genius," comparable gifts of controlled variety. When a personality has been perfected in this way the critic cannot meddle. He can only describe and perhaps—though I shall not attempt it here—find ways of appraising the merit of rival characters as one might judge the worth of rival candidates for friendship: Montaigne or Lamb, say, or E. B. White or E. M. Forster.

I have tried to suggest that there is in *The Citizen* at least as much artistic skill in the maker, and thus artistic pleasure for the receiver, as can be found in most novels, satires, plays, and poems of its period. I think a case could be made that it is Goldsmith's most important work, clearly outranking *The Vicar,* say, or *She Stoops to Conquer,* works that have had far more critical attention. I would also suggest that exemplars of this kind from other periods deserve more critical attention than we have given them. It is a curious literary kind, admittedly, neither highbrow nor lowbrow nor middlebrow nor even furrowedbrow. In every period it is enjoyed by a very broad range of readers, from those who are committed to high art to those who read little more than the daily papers and magazines where the columns appear: the "meridian" is often broad enough to include almost all readers for a given period. It can thus be even more interesting to cultural historians and sociologists than to critics. Perhaps no one will ever claim that its exemplars, even at their best, rival the greatest novels and plays and epic poems. But a good share of the world's imaginative genius has gone into their creation, and they surely deserve a criticism that can forget about demands for structural unity and attend to the self-portraiture of genius.

OLIVER W. FERGUSON

Antisentimentalism in Goldsmith's The Good Natur'd Man: *The Limits of Parody*

The traditional account of the English stage in the 1760s and 1770s as an arena for the contrasting types of comedy designated as "sentimental" and "laughing" includes at least three misreadings of the theatrical history of the period. The first two of these—that sentimental comedy was dominant and that it was displaced, at least temporarily, by the plays of Oliver Goldsmith and Richard Brinsley Sheridan—have been authoritatively corrected, though they may still be encountered. The third—that Goldsmith's earliest play, *The Good Natur'd Man,* was written as an attack on sentimental comedy— has not even been challenged. "Everyone knows," according to Robert Heilman, "that Goldsmith intended *The Good Natur'd Man* . . . as an answer to and criticism of the dominant sentimental comedy." Ricardo Quintana makes no claims for the dominance of either type, but he calls *The Good Natur'd Man* "an out-and-out satire of sentimental comedy." Earlier, Austin Dobson had said that Goldsmith's play was his "practical and individual protest against" the genre. And most recently G. S. Rousseau has assumed that "it was universally understood that Goldsmith's purpose in writing . . . [*The Good Natur'd Man* and *She Stoops to Conquer*] was to depose sentimental comedy from its stronghold."

To question this established opinion may seem perverse, or at the very least idle. Goldsmith, after all, is the author not only of the designedly antisentimenal *She Stoops to Conquer* but also of what has become the best-known critical attack on sentimental comedy in the eighteenth century,

From *The Dress of Words: Essays on Restoration and Eighteenth-Century Literature in Honor of Richmond P. Bond,* edited by Robert B. White, Jr. ©1978 by the University of Kansas Libraries.

An Essay on the Theatre. Furthermore, the accepted view of *The Good Natur'd Man* would seem to be justified by the play's theme and plot. Honeywood, the central character, is the victim of a compulsion to aid distress whenever he meets it. His benevolence, his anxiety to please everyone, and his refusal to allow uncomfortable realities to qualify his benign view of the world about him are pathological; and before the play is over, his "good nature" has almost destroyed him. However, because his faults arise from good will and are "so nearly allied to excellence," he is worth reclaiming. His uncle, Sir William Honeywood, who throughout the play has been "a concealed spectator of . . . [his nephew's] follies," contrives and then resolves difficulties that show the young man the dangers of his outlook and conduct. The final scene presents a chastened Honeywood in possession of fortune and true love and—most important—an intelligent attitude toward benevolence.

Honeywood's painfully acquired ethical view is obviously incompatible with the kind found in sentimental comedy. But it is the intentions governing Goldsmith's first comedy, not the fact of his antisentimentalism, that are in question. And the distinction is worth making, because the misunderstanding of Goldsmith's intentions in *The Good Natur'd Man* has resulted in a criticism that has not only been damaging to the play itself but has also affected the assessment of Goldsmith's seriousness as an opponent of the sentimental ethic. Some critics have argued that despite the professed theme of *The Good Natur'd Man,* the play's dénouement is no different from that of the typical sentimental comedy. The reclaimed and rewarded Honeywood, they say, is indistinguishable from the similarly redeemed dramas of the period. These same critics have pointed out various other details in the play which, considered along with its happy resolution, appear to support the charge that *The Good Natur'd Man* resembles the very sort of comedy it is supposed to be repudiating. As Arthur Friedman expressed this view in a recent essay, "Goldsmith's attack on the doctrine of good nature . . . is not so thoroughgoing an attack as at first it may seem."

Robert Heilman argued against this sort of criticism a generation ago. He had no difficulty in demonstrating Goldsmith's rejection of the worldview that obtains in the usual sentimental play. Because, however, he undertook his argument with the assumption that *The Good Natur'd Man* was a deliberate attack on sentimental comedy, he was also obliged to justify seemingly inconsistent details in the play and to account for the various features which Goldsmith's comedy has in common with the rival genre. He did so by arguing that these resemblances to sentimental comedy were intended "to provide the materials for satire." *The Good Natur'd Man,* in other words, attacks the genre by parodying it. This reading of Goldsmith's play has been most vigorously asserted in our day by Quintana, who insists that unless *The Good Natur'd Man* is recognized as a parody of sentimental comedy, it "becomes a rather silly and confused affair, *partaking unconsciously of the sentimentalism which it laughs at*" [my italics].

On the face of it, this is an attractive theory. It absolves Goldsmith from responsibility for any taint of sentimentalism in the play; indeed, it not only disinfects such suspected passages, it also endows them with the virtue of satiric intent. This interpretation does, however, raise some objections. For one, how is it that Goldsmith's contemporaries misunderstood his intentions on so crucial a point? Quintana assures us that eighteenth-century audiences mistakenly supposed "that the reform of the hero—from benevolism to anti-benevolism!—was intended to bring the play to a touching conclusion." Critics were similarly obtuse if the earliest reviews can be considered reliable. The reviewers for the *Monthly Review*, the *Critical Review*, the *London Magazine*, the *St. James's Chronicle*, and the *Gentleman's Magazine* reacted variously to Goldsmith's comedy; but they were apparently alike in their inability to understand it.

There is a more fundamental objection to reading *The Good Natur'd Man* as a parody, an objection that has to do with the nature, the uses, and the limits of parody itself. While it is capable of a number of variations, parody achieves its effects by means of incongruous imitation. One of the best examples in Goldsmith's work occurs in act 2 of *She Stoops to Conquer,* when the awkward Marlow stammers sentimental clichés to Kate Hardcastle. The situation itself is parodic: Marlow, who is brazenly assured around barmaids and servants but speechless in the presence of ladies of quality, is Goldsmith's comic version of that dramatic stereotype, the good-hearted rake. As Marlow attempts to engage in sentimental discourse with Kate, the dialogue of a typical sentimental comedy is parodied by the manner in which it is presented; and no one familiar with the serious model can be unaware of its comic distortion in Goldsmith's hands:

> MISS HARDCASTLE. I have often been surprised how a man of *sentiment* could ever admire those light airy pleasures, where nothing ever reaches the heart.
>
> MARLOW. It's—a disease—of the mind, madam. In the variety of tastes there must be some who wanting a relish—for—um—a—um.
>
> MISS HARDCASTLE. I understand you, sir. There must be some,

who wanting a relish for refined pleasures, pretend to de-
spise what they are incapable of tasting.
MARLOW. My meaning, madam, but infinitely better expressed.
And I can't help observing—a—
MISS HARDCASTLE. . . . You were going to observe, Sir—
MARLOW. I was observing, madam—I protest, madam, I forget
what I was going to observe.

Quintana bases his argument for a parodic reading of *The Good Natur'd Man* on the play's conclusion: "A life-long foe of literary sentimentalism," he writes, Goldsmith "could adopt the sentimental style when it served his purposes to do so—witness the dialogue that brings *The Good Natur'd Man,* an antisentimental comedy, to a familiarly sentimental close." When we turn to the scene, we indeed find the happy ending characteristic of sentimental comedies: Sir William points the moral of the tale; Honeywood acknowledges the error of his former way of life and is accordingly rewarded with Miss Richland, whom he has loved in silence for four acts; even a minor character, the scheming Lofty, announces his intention to reform. But when, following Quintana's suggestion, we examine the dialogue of the scene, we find Sir William lecturing Honeywood in these terms:

I own that a desire of correcting your follies led me hither. I saw, with indignation, the errors of a mind that only sought applause from others; that easiness of disposition, which, tho' inclin'd to the right, had not courage to condemn the wrong. I saw with regret those splendid errors, that still took name from some neighbouring duty. Your charity, that was but injustice; your benevolence, that was but weakness; and your friendship but credulity. I saw, with regret, great talents and extensive learning, only employed to add sprightliness to error, and encrease your perplexities. I saw your mind with a thousand natural charms: but the greatness of its beauty served only to heighten my pity for its prostitution.

And when Honeywood vows to mend his ways, he speaks in this vein:

Yes, Sir, I now too plainly perceive my errors. My vanity, in attempting to please all, by fearing to offend any. My meanness in approving folly, lest fools should disapprove. Henceforth, therefore, it shall be my study to reserve my pity for real distress; my friendship for true merit, and my love for her, who first taught me what it is to be happy.

Now, there is undeniably a resemblance between this stilted discourse and the dialogue of sentimental drama, but where are the telltale signs of parody—to say nothing of the *comedy* that we normally associate with the device? There are no clues in the style, the phrases and rhythms of Goldsmith's prose or the manner of its presentation: there is nothing here comparable to the sentimental dialogue between Marlow and Kate. Nor does the context of Honeywood's words suggest a parodic aim, as it did in the scene from *She Stoops to Conquer*. Nothing in the dramatic situation instructs us to read Sir William's and Honeywood's remarks as absurd. On the contrary, at this juncture of the play we expect speeches of this sort. If, then, this is a parody, how can we distinguish it from the genuinely sentimental scene? In what way is Goldsmith's imitation *incongruous*?

Quintana apparently feels that Goldsmith's inexperience as a dramatist was responsible for the failure of critics and audiences and readers to grasp his point. *The Good Natur'd Man*, he argues, is "badly faulted [because] . . . the true ironic intent of the entire piece remains masked throughout. . . . Goldsmith's . . . parody of the sentimental play comes so close to being the thing that it is deriding that it fails to make its point in the theatre, where too great a degree of subtlety is fatal." Goldsmith was beyond question inexperienced as a playwright when he wrote his first comedy. He had much to learn, and the distance between *The Good Natur'd Man* and *She Stoops to Conquer* must be measured in more than years. But Goldsmith also knew a great deal. After all, *The Good Natur'd Man* was written in the tenth year of an active, varied, and by that time highly successful literary career. Theatrical inexperience notwithstanding, the uses of parody were hardly unfamiliar to the author of *The Citizen of the World* and *The Vicar of Wakefield*.

For that matter there is one brief conversation in *The Good Natur'd Man* that does parody sentimental dialogue—too slight and incidental to the design of the scene to warrant reading the entire play as Goldsmith's ironic version of a sentimental comedy, but sufficient to demonstrate that in 1767 he knew how to write recognizable parody. In act 3 Honeywood is arrested for debt, and to keep this embarrassing circumstance from his friends, he passes the attending bailiffs off as visiting gentlemen. In the scene in which the bailiffs agree to cooperate with his scheme, there is this exchange:

HONEYWOOD. Tenderness is a virtue, Mr. Twitch.

BAILIFF. Ay, Sir, its a perfect treasure. I love to see a gentleman with a tender heart. I don't know, but I think I have a tender heart myself. If all that I have lost by my heart was put together, it would make a—but no matter for that.

HONEYWOOD. Don't account it lost, Mr. Twitch. The ingratitude
of the world can never deprive us of the conscious happiness
of having acted with humanity ourselves.

BAILIFF. Humanity, Sir, is a jewel. It's better than gold. I love
humanity. People may say, that we, in our way, have no
humanity; but I'll shew you my humanity this moment.
There's my follower here, little Flanigan, with a wife and
four children, a guinea or two would be more to him, than
twice as much to another. Now, as I can't shew him any
humanity myelf, I must beg leave you'll do it for me.

Here, as in the conversation between Marlow and Kate, Goldsmith is
mocking typical sentimental cant. Both the situation and the manner in
which the sentimental discourse is presented (the bailiff's mean appearance
and Twitch's inelegant accent) make the parody unmistakable. If Goldsmith
had had a similar aim in the final scene of the play, he had the ability to
make his point clear—and his parody funny.

The attempt to read the conclusion of *The Good Natur'd Man* as
Heilman and Quintana recommend extends the device of parody beyond
manageable limits. We are left uncertain not only how to differentiate the
play from unabashedly sentimental comedies but also how to read comparable modes of expression elsewhere in Goldsmith's works. Goldsmith could
and did, as Quintana says, adopt a sentimental style when it suited his
purpose, but he could also write at a rhetorical pitch that is often too high
for twentieth-century tastes. To label such passages as parody is to assume
a critical attitude that is anachronistic and presumptuous. A good example
(too long to quote here) of Goldsmith's high-flown style is the essay, "A City
Night-Piece." Here is a briefer illustration in the same vein: "As the reputation of books is raised not by their freedom from defect, but the greatness
of their beauties; so should that of men be prized not for their exemption
from fault, but the size of those virtues they are possessed of." This speech—
which sounds very like one of Sir William Honeywood's—is from *The Vicar
of Wakefield*. The speaker is Sir William Thornhill, whose role as deus ex
machina and exemplar of the novel's theme, is unambiguous. However
pompous they may sound, his words could not conceivably be read as
parody. Here is another example: "Charles, Charles, how hast thou deceived me." Again, however the words might seem to us to demand it, their
context makes a parodic reading impossible. The speaker is Marlow's father, and he utters the exclamation on finding his son wooing Kate, for

whom he had earlier expressed indifference. Parody here would be point-less; there is simply nothing in the dramatic situation to parody.

Passages of this sort can be found throughout Goldsmith's works. The reason is that Goldsmith was writing not parodically but stereotypically. An obvious characteristic of his prose style is the recurrence of common themes, approaches, and methods of development and of stereotyped words and expressions. An awareness of this fact should make us cautious with our generalizations about Goldsmith's parodic use of "sentimental style." In act 4 of *She Stoops to Conquer,* we know immediately that Marlow's "By heaven, she weeps," is parody, not because of what we might call the extravagant diction but because Marlow's words are inaccurate: he is de-ceived by the appearance of a Kate who, the stage directions tell us, is "pretending to cry." On the other hand, the elder Marlow's "How hast thou deceived me" is a stereotype. In *The Vicar of Wakefield,* Arabella Wilmot exclaims, "O goodness, how have I been deceived," as does Honeywood at the end of *The Good Natur'd Man.* In none of these in-stances does the situation or the manner of presentation alert us to a parodic intent.

When we recognize the frequency of such stereotyped phrases in Gold-smith's prose, we should not attach undue importance to passages which bear only a verbal resemblance to the language commonly found in plays and novels (sentimental or not) of the period. Instances of this sort in *The Good Natur'd Man* become even less significant (and interesting) when we realize that in writing the play, Goldsmith was concerned not with paro-dying sentimental drama but with treating in the form of a conventional comedy a subject of abiding interest to him: the dangers of untutored be-nevolence. As early as 1759, in a letter to his brother Henry, he described his situation in words that could have been uttered by Honeywood in the last scene of *The Good Natur'd Man:* "I had learn'd from books to love virtue, before I was taught from experience the necessity of being selfish. . . . and often, by being even from my narrow finances charitable to excess, I forgot the rules of justice, and placed myself in the very situation of the wretch who thank'd my bounty."

Goldsmith gave this problem literary expression in various genres throughout his career. Heilman noted its presence in the essay, "On Justice and Generosity"; and we see the theme exemplified by such characters as Asem the Man-hater, Sir William Thornhill, and Richard Nash. Of all Honeywood's antecedents, however, the most pertinent is found in *The Citizen of the World,* in the person of Mr. Drybone, the Man in Black—most pertinent because he, like Honeywood and unlike Nash or Asem or

Thornhill, is presented in comic terms. Reared by a foolish father to be "a mere machine of pity," Drybone is cast into a predatory world where he is an easy mark for everyone he encounters, all of whom exploit and then dismiss him with the contemptuous phrase that forms a litany throughout Drybone's recital of his history: "my friends were now perfectly satisfied that I was undone, and yet they thought it a pity for one who had not the least harm in him, and was so very good natured." The phrase and the condescending tone are echoed eight years later by two characters discussing Honeywood's impending ruin:

> LOFTY. The man, to be sure, was immensely good natur'd. But then I could never find that he had any thing in him.
> MRS. CROAKER. His manner, to be sure, was excessive harmless; some, indeed, thought it a little dull.

Because of the similarity in Goldsmith's handling of the same theme in *The Good Natur'd Man* and the history of the Man in Black, his resolution of Drybone's and Honeywood's dilemma is especially interesting. Although Drybone assures his companion that he has broken his habit of uncritical benevolence, we know from his actions and his companion's comments that his reformation is only professed, that "he is generous even to profusion," and that his charity is still "rather the effect of appetite than reason." Had Goldsmith intended the resolution of *The Good Natur'd Man* as a parody of the tidy and secure world of sentimental comedy, he could have achieved his aim effectively by treating Honeywood as he had done Drybone. But Honeywood's reformation is genuine, and there is no hint in our final view of him that it will not be lasting.

II

The assertion that Goldsmith designed *The Good Natur'd Man* as an antisentimental comedy was apparently first made by William Cooke in 1805: "Dr. Goldsmith was the first to attack [sentimental comedy], by his successive productions of *The Good Natur'd Man* and *She Stoops to Conquer*." Cooke's opinion would be of more value had it been delivered at some time nearer the theatrical season of 1768—or at least before the production of *She Stoops to Conquer*. Goldsmith's second comedy has had much to do with the accepted view of his intentions in his first. Two other compositions that have helped establish that view are the Preface to *The Good Natur'd Man* and, after the work was first attributed to Goldsmith in 1798, *An Essay on the Theatre*.

Goldsmith's preface to *The Good Natur'd Man,* which was written the evening the play opened at Covent Garden January 29, 1768, and published the following week, was occasioned by circumstances surrounding the production. The play was moderately successful. There was a fairly even mixture of favorable and unfavorable criticism in the newspapers and magazines, and by the end of the season there had been eleven performances. Goldsmith's pleasure in this success, however, was marred by two events. One was the notoriety which the play gained because of the bailiffs' scene. The first-night audience objected so strenuously to this instance of low comedy that Goldsmith was forced to delete the episode from subsequent performances. His anger at this incident was aggravated by the acclaim which had greeted another new comedy, Hugh Kelly's *False Delicacy.* Kelly's play had opened at Drury Lane a week earlier, and it was enjoying an extravagantly favorable reception.

False Delicacy is by no means uncritical of some of the excesses of sentimentalism. Nor is it devoid of laughter. It contains two humorous characters and some genuine, if not compelling, comic scenes. Nevertheless, it embodies all the signficant features of sentimental comedy, and it was for these that the reviewers were praising it. One, writing in the *St. James's Chronicle,* compared the new comedies playing at Covent Garden and Drury Lane, approving of both and noting their striking differences: "If the Drury-Lane Comedy is more refined, correct, and sentimental, the Covent-Garden performance is more bold, more comick, and more characteristic [i.e., presenting vivid characterization]." The reviewer congratulated the public for being "at once in possession of two such comedies," but Goldsmith did not share his sense of good fortune. Not only was the more successful play being applauded for precisely the qualities his own comedy lacked, but also his rivalry with Kelly was complicated by other factors. Goldsmith had first submitted his play to Garrick. It was only after Garrick's continued unwillingness either to accept or reject the manuscript that Goldsmith gave it to George Colman, the new manager at Covent Garden. Thus, even before the 1768 season opened, *False Delicacy* and *The Good Natur'd Man* were cast in competing roles. For a final complication in this chapter of theater history, until their public confrontation in 1768, Kelly and Goldsmith had been friends. The assessment of the situation by Goldsmith's biographer, Sir James Prior, is a triumph of understatement: "Two comedies appearing nearly at the same moment at the two houses, of professedly opposite styles and merits, necessarily involved a kind of rivalry between the authors; and the continual discussions to which they gave rise when theatrical affairs were of general interest, their publication within three days of each other, their progress step by step through the press, a fourth edition of each being called for about the same time, produced at length something like jealousy."

It is against this background that Goldsmith's preface must be read. The substance of the brief piece is in its first paragraph:

> When I undertook to write a comedy, I confess I was strongly prepossessed in favour of the poets of the last age, and strove to imitate them. The term, *genteel comedy,* was then unknown amongst us, and little more was desired by an audience, than nature and humour, in whatever walks of life they were more conspicuous. The author of the following scenes never imagined that more would be expected of him, and therefore to delineate character has been his principal aim. Those who know any thing of composition, are sensible, that in pursuing humour, it will sometimes lead us into the recesses of the mean; I was even tempted to look for it in the master of a spunging-house: but in deference to the public taste, grown of late, perhaps, too delicate; the scene of the bailiffs was retrenched with representation. In deference also to the judgment of a few friends, who think in a particular way, the scene is here restored. The author submits it to the reader in his closet; and hopes that too much refinement will not banish humour and character from our's, as it has already done from the French theatre. Indeed the French comedy is now become so very elevated and sentimental, that it has not only banished humour and *Moliere* from the stage, but it has banished all spectators too.

Though he does not mention Kelly's play, Goldsmith obviously has *False Delicacy* in mind as the kind of genteel comedy that threatens to banish humor from the stage. It is equally obvious that the preface is his direct response to the hostile reception given the now-restored bailiffs' scene on the opening night of *The Good Natur'd Man.* Arthur Murphy has fixed the time of composition precisely. The upper gallery, he recalled, hissed the scene, and "from that hiss Goldsmith was in the dining room of Griffin the Bookseller . . . madly appealing to Posterity. He had before him three different Prefaces, in all of them appealing to Posterity. He was in Great Distress of Mind. I told him that if He would Let me, I could Easily deliver him from his difficulties. . . . and accordingly I Extracted a *short sober Preface* out of his blotted Papers, and Left out the appeal to Posterity. He was very thankful." Given all the circumstances, it is hardly surprising that Goldsmith's preface is an aggressive defense of the rejected scene and that as such it is devoted exclusively to a justification of low comedy. When, five years later, Goldsmith wrote a play deliberately attacking sentimental comedy, his manner of proceeding was altogether different. In *An Essay on the Theatre,* written in preparation for the appearance of *She Stoops to Conquer,* he examined the various aspects of sentimental comedy—its rationale, its aim, its shallow characterization and empty dialogue, its proscription of low humor. It is this essay, and not the preface to *The Good Natur'd Man,* that has become the *locus classicus* for Goldsmith's opinion of laughing and sentimental comedy. Far from being a major statement of artistic intent, the earlier document is a narrowly limited occasional piece, prompted by commercial rivalry, envy, and chagrin.

III

To recognize that Goldsmith did not write *The Good Natur'd Man* as a satire on sentimental comedy will not obviate the play's faults. The unredeemable dullness of all the serious characters is the principal one, and there are others. They do not, however, include oversubtle parody or unconscious sentimentalism. There is no justification for calling *The Good Natur'd Man* a flawed attack on sentimental comedy. Still less will a recognition of Goldsmith's aim in his first play deny his consistent opposition to sentimental comedy. An author may choose to reject a literary style instead of parodying it.

If Goldsmith's play is read on its own terms and not as the opening shot in a battle against the sort of comedy represented by *False Delicacy,* it will be seen that *The Good Natur'd Man,* like Kelly's play, is a conventional specimen of English comedy in the third quarter of the eighteenth century. A good many of its so-called sentimental touches—stilted dialogue, the requisite happy ending abounding with good feelings and professions of good intentions—can be found in comedies of every variety in the period. Further, a number of these plays utilize, and not as parody, aspects of both laughing and sentimental comedy: Kelly's satire on *false* delicacy has been noted by more than one critic, none of whom has termed the play an antisentimental comedy! As the early history of *False Delicacy* and *The Good Natur'd Man* demonstrates, two essentially different kinds of comedy—one laughing, the other sentimental—were placed in deliberate and direct competition during the 1768 season. Kelly's was an enormous success. Its ridicule of false delicacy gave no offense. *The Good Natur'd Man,* on the other hand, received notably harsh treatment from the first-night audience and from some of the reviewers not because it attacked sentimental comedy but because of the unacceptable low humor of the bailiffs' scene. Had Goldsmith not written this offending scene, the initial reception of his play would have been markedly different. When, three years later, he began work on a second comedy, the events of early 1768—Kelly's success and his own humiliation—were clear and bitter in Goldsmith's memory. *She Stoops to Conquer* was his cheerful revenge for the injuries done *The Good Natur'd Man*.

ROGER LONSDALE

"A Garden, and a Grave":
The Poetry of Oliver Goldsmith

Oliver Goldsmith remains notoriously the most elusive person in the otherwise voluminously documented Johnson circle, no less a puzzle to the modern biographer than he appears to have been to his contemporaries. And if the appearance of Arthur Friedman's edition of the *Collected Works* has imposed some order on what had been a confusingly miscellaneous literary output, Goldsmith's place in eighteenth-century literary history, whether as satirist or sentimentalist, as late neoclassicist or proto-romantic, seems to be a subject which still offers plenty of scope for discussion.

In one area, however, that of his two most ambitious poems, agreement appears to have been reached during the last decade. Ricardo Quintana's essay on *The Deserted Village* in 1964, a corrective to naïve interpretations of the poem as an emotional utterance by Goldsmith himself, stressed instead its rhetorical artistry, in which the "I" in the poem is a point of view manipulated by the poet like a character in a play, by no means to be confused with the "real" Goldsmith. "After all, Goldsmith was an Augustan," Quintana declares, and to the Augustans, who thought in terms only of general human experience, direct self-revelation was foreign. Later critics have elaborated this rhetorical emphasis. Richard Eversole has argued that in *The Deserted Village* the "disposition of thought conforms to the structural rules of a classical oration" and, with the assistance of Cicero and Quintilian (and, some may think, Procrustes), has discovered a traditional seven-part rhetorical structure in the poem. We are to consider its

From *The Author in His Work: Essays on a Problem in Criticism*, edited by Louis L. Martz and Aubrey Williams. © 1978 by Yale University. Yale University Press, 1978.

apparently personal emotion, its sentimentalism, as no more than a device
to persuade the poet's audience to agree with his political thesis.

Leo F. Storm has gone even further in detaching the poet from his
poem. Not merely is the sentimental aspect "a conscious rhetorical device
for heightening the drama of the poem rather than . . . a revelation of Goldsmith's personal stress of feeling": even its ideas, the earnest condemnation
of luxury and its attendant social evils, need not be thought of as convictions seriously held by Goldsmith himself, in a poem the basic concern of
which was merely "to defend the conservative social order." Formally the
poem blends aspects of the English georgic and of topographical poetry, and
exploits the stock emotional and intellectual associations of these familiar
genres for the rhetorical purpose of dramatizing a degenerating society.
R. J. Jaarsma has also argued that *The Deserted Village* must be understood
as "a kind of poetry that exercises a deliberative control over its material."
The view that the poem "is a kind of *cri de coeur* may safely be dismissed":
Goldsmith is no "romantic, longing for a return to thoughtless innocence,"
nor is Auburn the recreation "of a lonely mind almost drowned by waves of
sentimentalism." The essence of the poem is its protest against the destruction of humanistic social values and Auburn is merely a device to reveal the
glaring impotency of modern social progress. The eviction of Goldsmith
from his poetry was completed in 1969 by Robert H. Hopkins, in the course
of an elaborate discussion of *The Traveller*. On no account is the "I" in the
poem to be equated with Goldsmith himself. Quotations from Aristotle's
Rhetoric enable us to understand that the persona's appeals to our pity and
sympathy are merely devices to condition us to the political argument of a
poem which cannot "be legitimately read as autobiographical statement,"
but "must be viewed in the objective context of rhetoric."

Such unanimous disapproval of any tendency to an autobiographical
reading of Goldsmith's poetry might be interpreted as an indirect tribute to
the strength of the temptation to indulge in it. Nineteenth-century readers of
Goldsmith, of course, surrendered enthusiastically to that temptation, for
The Traveller and *The Deserted Village* seemed to lend themselves better
than most Augustan poetry to a demand for a close and "sincere" relationship between the poem and the poet's personal life. Sir James Prior, Goldsmith's biographer, found in *The Deserted Village* "those personal allusions
that always add to the interest of a poem." For Washington Irving, the
poem was "truly . . . a mirror of the author's heart and of all the fond
pictures of early friends and early life for ever present there." Thackeray
described Goldsmith as "the most beloved of English writers," explaining
that "Your love of him is half pity," pity for "the career, the sufferings, the

genius, the gentle nature" of "this honest soul" as revealed directly in *The Deserted Village,* in which "the whole character of the man is told." Far from finding him elusive, the nineteenth-century reader was confident that Goldsmith spoke spontaneously and openly of his own life and sorrows in the poetry, the very absence of precise biographical information about the man only encouraging this belief. In 1900 Henry James summed up the attitude of the previous century to *The Vicar of Wakefield* in terms which apply equally well to the poetry:

> The books that live, apparently, are very personal. . . . The author of this one never, at any rate, lets go our hand; and we, on our side, keep hold with a kind of sense, which is one of the most touching things our literature gives us, of all that, by doing so, we make up to him for.
>
> (Introduction to *The Vicar of Wakefield,* 1900)

Goldsmith's reputation was probably at its highest when he could inspire in his readers this response of mingled love and pity to a curious entanglement of himself and his writings. The corrective emphasis of modern criticism was desperately needed if greater eighteenth-century poets than Goldsmith, notably Pope, were to be appreciated. It is unnecessary to chart the process by which the poet has been separated from his poem, a process aided by influential theories of authorial impersonality, the distinction between "the man who suffers" and "the mind which creates," the weighting of tradition or sociology against the individual talent, and a renewed emphasis on rhetoric and the persona. In the crucial reappraisal of Pope, there has been no more influential essay than Maynard Mack's "The Muse of Satire" (*Yale Review* 41, 1951), which insisted on the traditional aspects of his satiric voice, on the distinction between the historical and the dramatic Pope. More recently, in *The Garden and the City,* Mack has brilliantly analyzed the dramatic figure who speaks in Pope's later satires to demonstrate the blending of the personal experiences of the "real" Pope of Twickenham with features deriving from Roman models and seventeenth-century retirement literature. Mack declares at once that he is offering literary history and biography rather than criticism, from which the former are "more or less separable." Yet the effect of his demonstration of the complexity of the poetic Pope should be a deterrent not merely to those who would make simple assumptions about poetry as self-expressive, but, implicitly at least, to those who would confine themselves at the other extreme to a strictly rhetorical approach.

The self-dramatization in Pope's later poetry, a fact hardly digested in our generalizations about his age, might be considered a unique case, since he could blend traditional and rhetorical elements with a level of personal experience which was verifiable, not merely retrospectively, but by his original audience. Pope's contemporaries did not and could not venture so far: the "I" in their poetry, if projected at all, speaks either as a virtually anonymous, judicious intelligence, who can count on the agreement of the reasonable members of his audience, or as a traditional poetic personality, adopting standard and recognizable genre guises, or as an ironically but unambiguously impersonated mask. When, as is evidently the case with Goldsmith, the poetic "I" seems to speak more idiosyncratically, especially when projecting a problematically suffering self, we can either decide that this is a different kind of poetry (the currently unfashionable resort to Pre-Romanticism), or seek some way of accommodating the phenomenon to the assumption that all eighteenth-century poetry is public, traditional, and formally contrived. If such "sentimentalism" cannot be identified as ironic (the preferred solution), the alternative is to categorize it as rhetorical. The rhetorical "I," as we have seen, remains essentially impersonal, an emotional self projected merely for persuasive purposes, its only function to alter the reader's opinion.

Apart from avoiding simpleminded reading of the poetry as autobiographical statement, the rhetorical approach has a further advantage. Sentimental or didactic aspects of the "I," which would be unattractive or unconvincing if attributed directly to the poet himself, are apparently acceptable if they can be thought of as part of a quasi-theatrical performance by a manipulated poetic self. The limitation of the approach, however, is simply the nature of the questions it begs, its sweeping identification, for example, of Goldsmith as securely "Augustan" in his poetic habits and intentions, and its assumptions about the static nature of eighteenth-century poetry. The evidence suggests that, on the contrary, by the mid-century a number of poets were fumbling in various ways to discover a personal voice which could not be reduced simply to the anonymous, traditional, or rhetorical. I have attempted elsewhere, no doubt temerariously in the present climate, to trace some features of Thomas Gray's tentative search for acceptable poetic means of speaking of personal experience, in an age which officially doubted its interest or value. The case of Goldsmith might also deserve reconsideration, to discover whether the attraction of the rhetorical approach is also its limitation, its fastidious distaste for what is likely to be disconcertingly messy: the complex possibility that the increasingly obtrusive "I" in later eighteenth-century poetry is combining traditional features and rhetorical habits with genuinely self-expressive intentions.

The evidence must ultimately be the poetry itself, and the exercise proposed is not the traditional pursuit of literal parallels with Goldsmith's biography. Yet since the rhetorical approach rests on crucial if implicit assumptions about Goldsmith's intentions, evidence about his attitude to his own poetry might have clarified the situation. Most of what we know about the man, however, in the years in which he wrote *The Traveller* (1764) and *The Deserted Village* (1770), derives from Boswell's far from sympathetic depiction of him, from a few uninformative letters, and from a fund of usually farcical or dubious anecdotes. There is more striking and consistent evidence, about his personality at least, in the previous decade, the years following his departure from Ireland, in the letters he wrote to relatives and friends, whether they are read as directly confessional or as in themselves "rhetorical" attempts at persuasion (self-justification, appeals for money or sympathy). Throughout these early years in Edinburgh, Holland, and London, Goldsmith—often well aware of the "egotism" of his letters—is preoccupied with his loneliness, poverty, social inferiority, and unprepossessing appearance and manner. Melancholy, self-derisive, with a frustrated sense of his own talents, resentful of the contempt which he has habitually received—whether in Ireland, in spite of his nostalgia for it, or in his first years in London, because of those Irish origins themselves—the young Goldsmith is a strikingly self-conscious and self-absorbed figure, even, or perhaps especially, when indulging in humorous but intense fantasies about his future fame. As early as 1753 there is a revealing echo of Gray's *Elegy,* published only two years earlier: "Poverty, hopeless poverty, was my lot, and Melancholy was beginning to make me her own." The echo betrays the attraction of the figure of Gray's isolated, melancholy, doomed poet in that conclusion to the *Elegy* which Goldsmith would later particularly praise as "pathetic and interesting."

There is at times a curious and in some ways gratuitous transference of this awkwardly self-conscious self into the literary personality projected in Goldsmith's early miscellaneous prose, as in the anxious, blundering self which admits its own self-conscious pretense of ease and impudence in the introduction to his short-lived periodical *The Bee* in 1759. (Goldsmith was fascinated by distinguished men—Samuel Butler, Berkeley, Boyle, Pope—whose genius was belied by an unattractive appearance or awkward manner.) The self, when it obtrudes, is always problematic: "when we talk of ourselves, Vanity or Resentment have always too much to say," he commented cryptically at the very end of his series of "Chinese Letters" in *The Public Ledger.* Yet when collecting these essays as *The Citizen of the World*

in 1762, Goldsmith spoke openly, if anonymously, in his introduction about
his isolation and frustration:

> But at present I belong to no particular class. I resemble one of
> those solitary animals, that has been forced from its forest to
> gratify human curiosity. My earliest wish was to escape un-
> heeded through life; but I have been set up for half-pence, to fret
> and scamper at the end of my chain. Tho' none are injured by my
> rage, I am naturally too savage to court any friends by fawning.
> Too obstinate to be taught new tricks; and too improvident to
> mind what may happen, I am appeased, though not contented.
> Too indolent for intrigue, and too timid to push for favour, I
> am—But what signifies what am I.

One of the essays in *The Citizen of the World* describes a poet reading
to a club of authors an epic poem which, he explains, is "an heroical
description of nature. . . . The poem begins with the description of an author's bed-chamber: the picture was sketched in my own apartment; for you
must know, gentlemen, that I am myself the heroe." The enterprise is clearly
preposterous, yet rather, one suspects, because of its incongruous heroic
pretensions than because of its author's impulse to describe himself and his
own humble circumstances. Goldsmith had in fact sent a version of these
lines in 1759 to his brother Henry and, in spite of their ostensibly comic
purpose, their resemblance to his own situation at that time has been noted.
The complexity of his attitude to the poet's self-centered epic is suggested by
the fact that he later adapted the lines as part of his depiction of the humble
happiness of Auburn in *The Deserted Village*.

There is little that is heroic about Goldsmith's own life. In spite of his
later literary success, his financial incompetence meant that he was almost
continuously dependent on the booksellers for a living. Even if his early
distaste for the mere "compilations" of others—as opposed to true scholarship—necessarily modified as he himself attempted to justify the popu-
larizing historical, literary, and scientific compilations of his later years, it is
hard to believe that he viewed these profitable enterprises with any deep
satisfaction. Goldsmith was also sensitive enough to know very well that his
contemporaries to the end of his life saw him, with attitudes ranging from
the amicably patronizing to the contemptuous, as a somewhat ludicrous
figure. Biographically, his two major poems, both written with painstaking
care and with no immediate financial motive, almost certainly represent
what he himself considered the only true manifestations of his literary in-

tegrity and talent. In that sense their function was that they should deserve his own respect and demand that of the literary world.

II

As we approach his poetry, it would simplify matters if it were clear that Goldsmith, the impersonal rhetorical strategist of the modern critics, had in practice any enthusiasm for the art. On the contrary, in reviews and essays Goldsmith repeatedly attacked the assumptions of formal rhetoric, especially as employed in instruction in oratory. The terms in which he does so, sometimes with the aid of the *Encyclopédie*, are clearly as relevant to writing as to oratory. In *The Bee* he mocks the "pedants" who:

> Have ranged under proper heads, and distinguished with long learned names, *some* of the strokes of nature, or of passion, which orators have used. I say only *some* for a folio volume could not contain all the figures which have been used by the truly eloquent, and scarce a good speaker or writer, but makes use of some that are peculiar or new.

In his subsequent discussion of the inadequacies of English preaching, he demands a greater appeal to the passions of a popular audience, "not by the labours of the head, but the honest spontaneous dictates of the heart." The fervor and spontaneity of the preaching of the Methodists, of whom Goldsmith has otherwise a low opinion, explain their greater effectiveness. In another attack on rhetoric, he mentions the two ancients recently enlisted by critics to enable us to read his own poetry:

> These strong and vigorous emotions, therefore, can be no where taught, but they may be extinguished by rule; and this we find actually to have been the case; we find no Grecian orator truly sublime after the precepts of Aristotle, nor Roman after the lectures of Quintilian.

Goldsmith's objections spring from a deeper source than dislike of rhetorical figures. They are directed against assumptions calculated to inhibit the speaker or writer, to obstruct communication between the natural emotions of the orator or poet and the hearts of the audience, and to falsify the true voice of feeling. Within the limits of the critical vocabulary available to him, his views on poetry are consistent with this position.

It might no doubt be argued that Goldsmith's own poetry merely displays a "rhetoric" of sincerity and spontaneous emotion and that he would still expect his reader to respond to the "I" in his poetry as to a dramatic performer manipulated by a real and unaccountable Goldsmith in the background. A neglected comment on Savage's *The Bastard* in 1767 makes clear that Goldsmith did not take for granted that poetry must be read in this way:

> Almost all things written from the heart, as this certainly was, have some merit. The poet here describes sorrows and misfortunes which were by no means imaginary; and, thus, there runs a truth of thinking through this poem, without which it would be of little value, as Savage is, in other respects, but an indifferent poet.

Even if Goldsmith's response to the poem must have been reinforced by Johnson's moving *Life of Savage,* the attraction of the poetry of sincerity, grounded in real experience, is clear. The comment on Savage also clarifies Goldsmith's aims in the poem he had himself published three years earlier.

The dedications to his two major poems deserve particular attention, for they provide the best guidance we will obtain about the response Goldsmith hoped for. In the first state of the first edition of *The Traveller,* published in December 1764, the dedication consists of a single sentence, inscribing the poem to the Reverend Henry Goldsmith (a clergyman in Ireland) from "his most affectionate brother, Oliver Goldsmith." In the second state, which appeared shortly afterwards, Goldsmith's name was placed for the first time on the title page of one of his works, and the dedication was greatly expanded.

Goldsmith now explains the propriety of the affectionate dedication to his own brother by the fact that "a part of this Poem was formerly written to you from Switzerland." The subsequently verifiable fact that Goldsmith had indeed travelled in Switzerland some ten years earlier is less relevant than what he was choosing to emphasize to his original readers: that his poem had a genuine autobiographical basis. In other words, the poet within the poem, seated on a mountain in Switzerland and addressing his brother, is equated with the real Goldsmith who addresses his brother Henry in his dedication to the poem. Goldsmith emphasizes his brother's humble and pious life *because* of its relevance to his poem: "It will also throw a light upon many parts of it, when the reader understands that it is addressed to a man, who, despising Fame and Fortune, has retired early to Happiness and Obscurity, with an income of forty pounds a year." Henry's "sacred office," his humble but useful life as a clergyman, is contrasted with those who labor in "the field of Ambition," and of all kinds of ambition "that which pursues poetical fame, is the wildest." Goldsmith's own poem is thus deliberately characterized as a manifestation of such rash ambition, rash because of the factors which, as he goes on to explain, threaten true poetry: over-refinement in the arts, which has led "the powerful" to neglect poetry for painting and music; learned criticism, mistakenly seeking to "improve" poetry by emphasis on its self-conscious technical aspects; and partisan politics, which have made crude political satire (presumably that of Churchill) fashionable. Goldsmith's own aim is to moderate political hostility, by showing that equal happiness can exist under different forms of government and that any principle of happiness can be carried to excess. Such an aim, implicitly, is not merely for the good of the nation: Goldsmith has said enough to suggest that he is also concerned to create the conditions in which his own poetry would be appreciated.

It would be naïve to read *The Traveller* as a literal outpouring by the "real" Goldsmith, just as it would be rash to ignore conventional elements in the presentation of the "I" in the poem. Yet it is hard to see what more Goldsmith could have done to place his poem in an autobiographical context and to verify it as a genuine autobiographical utterance. Efforts to relate the poem to established genres usually relapse into gestures towards pastoral, georgic, and topographical poetry, ignoring the fact that it is a verse epistle addressed by Goldsmith to his own brother. Such verse epistles from abroad, as Dodsley's *Collection* indicates, form a recognizable subgenre in the period, and at times *The Traveller* echoes earlier poetic contrasts of European nations with each other or with Britain. What is impossible to ignore, both in the dedication and in the poem itself, is the enlargement of the decorously personal but non-self-revelatory element in the traditional verse epistle, to the point where the reader could hardly avoid feeling that, as Goldsmith would later say of Savage's poem, "the poet here describes sorrows and misfortunes which were by no means imaginary." The point may seem an elementary one: and yet Hopkins's elaborate analysis of the poem neglects the dedication, repeatedly insists that the "I" in the poem is "not to be equated with Goldsmith," that it cannot "legitimately be read as an autobiographical statement" but "must be viewed in the objective context of rhetoric," ignores the presence of the brother within the poem, and looks instead to Aristotle for guidance in responding to it.

The proof sheets of the poem show that it was originally to have been called *A Prospect of Society*. When published, it was entitled *The Traveller, or A Prospect of Society,* a sufficient indication that the narrator himself was to be as much the subject as its political content. The expansion of the dedication continues the process to the extent of informing the reader that the "I" in the poem *was* to be equated with Goldsmith himself. A sentence in the dedication later omitted, no doubt because of its slightly ludicrous implications, still indicates Goldsmith's frustration at the difficulty of speaking directly to the hearts of his readers, a situation oddly recreated by a rhetorical reading of the poem: "Though the poet were as sure of his aim as the imperial archer of antiquity, who boasted that he never missed the heart; yet would many of his shafts now fly at random, for the heart is too often in the wrong place."

Yet examination of the poem itself may suggest that Goldsmith had in fact underestimated the problems created by his personal presence in the poem and that he found it difficult to draw the poetic self and its predicament into a coherent relationship with his philosophic and political concerns. He was seeking a response from both the head and the heart of his reader, and his success in unifying it is limited. The opening of *The Traveller* draws at once on the situation established in the dedication. No convention would seem to account for the emphatic portrayal in lines 1–10, with their suspended syntax and weighty movement, of the poet as a melancholy, friendless wanderer against a broad European background, a "houseless stranger" whose heart turns "with ceaseless pain" to his brother. Indeed, this deeply personal note will be convincing enough to call into question the authority of any other tones the poet may subsequently adopt. Lines 11–22 endow the dwelling of the poet's brother, his "earliest friend," with overtones of sanctity and blessedness. Yet from such humble happiness, benevolence, and hospitality, which he once shared, the poet is mysteriously but emphatically excluded (ll. 23–30). His predicament of lonely wandering, of exile from the "blest . . . spot," is unexplained: he is passively "destin'd" and "impell'd" by "fortune" to wander and yet to "find no spot of all the world my own."

At line 31 the poet's utterance is fixed in time and place: "Even now, where Alpine solitudes ascend," he sits for "a pensive hour . . . / . . . above the storm's career," to look down upon the "hundred realms" visible below him. This elevated perspective, even if only a temporary respite, marks the moment of attempted conversion of the exiled wanderer's unhappy isolation into a traditional philosophical detachment. Yet Goldsmith finds it no easy matter to make sense of the poetic self's spiritual exhaustion, to construe such deprivation in acceptable terms (ll. 37–50). To "repine" amidst such "store"—"Creation's charms" as embodied in the prospect before him—would be "thankless pride" towards the beneficent Creator. Apparently it is the poet's "philosophical mind" which is in danger of arrogantly disdaining the satisfactions ordained by Providence for ordinary men. If the narrator's predicament is hardly elucidated, it is now possible that by leaving the "blest . . . spot," his brother's household, he himself disdained those "little things" which "are great to little men." The philosophical compensation ought to be, as the poet knows, that kind of cosmopolitan sympathy which "Exults in all the good of all mankind," as Lien Chi Altangi had earlier explained in *The Citizen of the World*: "The philosopher, who extends his regard to all mankind, must have still a smaller concern for what has already affected or may hereafter affect himself; the concerns of others make his whole study, and that study is his pleasure." Lines 45–50 accordingly rehearse, in what is in effect a form of serious parody, the conviction that a proper sense of the blessings of Creation on all men is a sufficient compensation for the poet's private sorrows.

Yet the apostrophic style of these lines betrays the uneasiness of the effort to move from self-absorption into philosophic sympathy with the good of mankind, to accept that, even if there is "no spot of all the world my own" (l. 30), it is consolation enough to find that "the world, the world is mine" (l. 50). The following paragraph (ll. 51–62) admits as much. An apparently querulous voice in the harmony of man, nature and God regularly celebrated by his contemporaries, the poet compares himself to a "lone miser," who rejoices in heaven's blessings, but still sighs and yearns for more. At first the simile seems to characterize the poet's own lonely longing as unattractively selfish and even obsessive. Hopkins sees it only as an effective rhetorical anticipation of the poem's main concern, its "indictment of laissez faire political economy," and quotes at length from Malachy Postlethwayt, a contemporary economist, to illustrate the age's attitude to the evils of hoarding. Goldsmith's own views on misers might seem more relevant. On at least three occasions in the *The Bee* he had argued that misers, who "have been described as madmen, who, in the midst of abundance, banish every pleasure, and make, from imaginary wants, real necessities," have been misrepresented by "the vain and idle." They are usually "Men who, by frugality and labour, raise themselves above their equals, and contribute their share of industry to the common stock." Indeed, "it were well, had we more misers than we have among us. I know few characters more useful in society."

Such passages should not merely correct facile assumptions about Goldsmith's economic views but emphasize the dangers of making all elements of a poem rhetorically subservient to some sweepingly defined purpose. And yet, whatever Goldsmith's own views, to choose to present the poetic self through the traditionally despised figure of the miser is an acknowledgment of the dubious respectability of self-absorbed introspection and betrays Goldsmith's difficulty in giving the narrator's private predicament, the lonely yearning of the miser, a more acceptable meaning. What is in fact offered is an unexpected version of Pope's "Self-love and Social [are] the same." Just as the misunderstood miser, according to *The Bee,* serves society, it turns out that the poet's sorrow is not after all self-absorbed:

> Yet oft a sigh prevails, and sorrows fall,
> To see the hoard of human bliss so small;
> And oft I wish, amidst the scene, to find
> Some spot to real happiness consign'd,
> Where my worn soul, each wand'ring hope at rest,
> May gather bliss to see my fellows blest.
>
> (ll. 57–62)

The poet's apparent ingratitude is on behalf of mankind. The "sympathetic mind" is unable to rejoice with conviction in the general good when mankind is still relatively so unblessed. We will be given no more adequate explanation of the poet's lonely wanderings and "worn soul" than this: that he is seeking, on behalf of mankind, the good society in which his own "real" happiness will be to recognize that of others.

What is puzzling about this explanation is that the poet had seemed in the opening lines to have identified just such a "blest . . . spot" in his brother's household: its unexplained inaccessibility makes its existence only the more obtrusive. Similarly, in the next two paragraphs (ll. 63–80), the cosmopolitan poet's mild irony against the narrowly "patriotic" instinct which leads all men to describe their own as "the happiest spot" is itself ironically qualified by his own original painful recognition that "His first best country ever is at home." Furthermore, the patriotic delusion, man's very ability to adapt to extremes of climate, is clearly in itself a kind of happiness, as Goldsmith's later discussion of different nations will show. The irony turns inadvertently back on the disabled poet-philosopher: to travel in search of happiness is only to equip oneself to assess the limitations of the happiness of others, and to lose one's own capacity for it.

Such ironies, springing from the poet's own conspicuous presence as melancholy seeker of happiness, seem to have been too complex or involuntary to sustain. Not surprisingly, Goldsmith starts to play down the subjective aspect. Suddenly it is "we," not "I," who "roam" and "compare" the blessings of different nations (ll. 73–75) and whose "wisdom" (l. 77) will in due course arrive at judicious conclusions about them. Yet even as the poet begins to adopt the tone of a confident lecturer ("But let us try these truths with closer eyes," l. 99) addressing a larger and more representative audience than his brother, he must attempt to dispose of the problematic, suffering self:

> Here for a while my proper cares resign'd,
> Here let me sit in sorrow for mankind,
> Like you neglected shrub, at random cast,
> That shades the steep, and sighs at every blast.
>
> (ll. 101–4)

Hopkins's comment that "rhetorically" the simile "reminds the reader again of the tone that the narrator holds toward the argument which he presents" seems curiously uninformative. The lines make clear that the poet's idiosyncratic sorrows, his "proper cares," are after all obstinately distinct from his generous "sorrow for mankind," reversing the fusion attempted in lines 57–62; and we are reminded that they will be ignorable only "for a while." To go on to describe that aspect of the self which remains as a neglected, sighing shrub, cast at random on the hillside, is almost ostentatiously to insist on the unhappy private predicament of the judicious surveyor of nations who now takes over the poem.

The following survey of Italy, Switzerland, France, and Holland (ll. 105–316), in which Goldsmith reveals considerable descriptive power and some epigrammatic talent, need not be followed in detail. The assessment of the happiness of each country, and the argument that each tends to concentrate dangerously on some favorite happiness (as if by some national ruling passion), are, in tone at least, objective and judicious. The symmetry of the balancing of the effects of nature and art in each society, and of the contrast between the different nations, supports the authoritative tone. At line 313, however, the poet begins once again to obtrude emotionally, his agitation proceeding from his concern at the state of Britain, where, while the climate is mild, the extremes lie in the proud, rational, freedom-loving, self-venerating British themselves. The blessings of British freedom are balanced by evils: proud self-dependence leads to neglect of natural and social claims, even to conflict, ferment, and faction. The natural "bonds" which should link men in harmony are replaced by enslaving "bonds" of wealth and law (ll. 349–60). Unexpectedly, the first victims of this dangerous situation in Britain are "talent" and "merit" (l. 354). The reference to poets who once, with reasonable expectations, "wrote for fame" (l. 358) recalls the contrast in the dedication between the wild ambition of seeking poetical fame and Henry Goldsmith's humble retirement from the world. The threats to poetry described in the dedication, over-refinement and political faction, are apparently identical with the evils which threaten the national well-being in the poem itself.

If the emotional "I" who returns at line 361 is no longer the detached, judicious lecturer on European nations, he is still on the whole distinct from the passive and mysterious sufferer of the opening of the poem. His emotion is that of apparently justified indignation at identifiable evils. The exclusion of the more problematic self is enacted in a revision Goldsmith made at this point. The poet denies (ll. 361–62) that, by stressing the dangers of Freedom, he intends to flatter the monarchy or the aristocracy. In the first edition, he had gone on to exclaim, "Perish the wish; for, inly satisfy'd, /Above their pomps I hold my ragged pride." The poet's "ragged pride" too obtrusively detracted from the authority of the analyst of Britain's ills, awkwardly recalling the friendless wanderer of the poem's opening, who had seemed anything but "inly satisfy'd," and the couplet was removed. Otherwise, the mounting emotion at this stage of the poem recalls the fervent (and more embittered) indignation of Pope's later satires, as the poet's normally "Calm . . . soul" (l. 379) is roused by such evils as aristocratic contention for power at the expense of the monarchy and control of the law by the rich.

At line 393 the poet once more addresses Henry Goldsmith ("Yes, brother, curse with me"), as if seeking to establish some connection between the personal sorrow focused initially on his brother's dwelling and his present state of patriotic indignation, which has led him, somewhat self-consciously, to "Tear off reserve, and bare my swelling heart" (l. 390). Hitherto his concern at the state of Britain has noticeably failed to embody itself in any single, expressive visual image. Now the poet deplores the triumph of wealth in Britain by defining it as the exchange of her "useful sons" as colonists for the "useless ore" of foreign luxuries (ll. 397–98). The following description of opulence maintaining her grandeur by depopulating villages (ll. 401–12), as is well known, anticipates the elaborate treatment of the subject in *The Deserted Village*. The poet's anguished, sympathetic imagination visualizes the innocent villagers as passive exiles in a savage colonial America (ll. 413–22), "even now" entangled in dangerous forests, threatened by savage beasts, murderous Indians, and violent storms, surrounded by "distressful yells":

> The pensive exile, bending with his woe,
> To stop too fearful, and too faint to go,

> Casts a long look where England's glories shine,
> And bids his bosom sympathize with mine.
>
> (ll. 419–22)

The last line is unexpected. Surely it is the poet's role to sympathize with the exiled villager? Obviously, the pensive exile may well share the poet's outraged conviction that "England's glories" are ill-purchased at the cost of such suffering. Yet the line seems to mean more: that the nature of the suffering of the poet and the exile is identical. The private predicament of the opening of the poem, consciously set aside in its "philosophical" center, has reemerged, validated by patriotic indignation, to project itself into the fate of the villagers, a nightmare version of the poet's own exile. The equation of the "pensive exile" in America with the mysteriously deprived poet, who is spending a "pensive hour" on a mountain to utter this meditation, is even clearer in the earliest version of line 422, in which the villager "gives his griefs to sympathize with mine." The inaccessibility of his brother's happy dwelling to the poet, puzzling in the literally autobiographical terms invoked by Goldsmith himself, is half-explained by its imaginative equation with the once happy but depopulated village later in the poem. But what also emerges is that, like the villager, the poet's more immediate exile is caused by his rejection from a society increasingly dominated by wealth and political faction, a spiritual alienation from a Britain inimical to poetry itself and the values on which it depends. The threats to poetry, as outlined in the dedication, are also those which depopulate villages.

Goldsmith may well have intended to conclude the poem with this only half-articulated identification of poet and villager. The earliest version of the poem, *A Prospect of Society*, ends at this point, and it is likely that it was Samuel Johnson who insisted on a more lucid and orthodox resolution and, indeed, wrote half of the final paragraph. Goldsmith, however, begins it: "Vain, very vain, my weary search to find / That bliss which only centers in the mind" (ll. 423–24). Divergence between the problematic and judicious selves in the poem is reflected in the two possible readings of this couplet, which presumably means that the search for anything other than inner happiness is vain but half-admits that, in the poet's own case, the search for inner happiness is itself futile. Under Johnson's influence any such wavering is only momentary, and the poem concludes in a mood of resolute Christian stoicism, Johnson himself contributing all but two of the last ten lines. Although there may be terrors and tyrannies under any form of government, they hardly affect the happiness, the "domestic joy," of the individual, "which no loud storms annoy." Perhaps echoing the original search for "a spot" which the poet could call "my own" (l. 30), Johnson ends the poem by insisting that "reason, faith and conscience" are "all our own" (l. 438).

Hopkins, admitting the difficulty created by this antipolitical conclusion to a supposedly rhetorical political poem, concludes that the poet has resolved to be "inner-directed": when "cohesive government fails" the individual must find happiness in his own virtue. The effect of Johnson's conclusion is, however, emphatically different: that such matters as "cohesive government" are *irrelevant* to the individual. It is far from clear, indeed, what the poet himself resolves—in his own person he ends with a baffled question (ll. 425–26)—or, moreover, what inner or external resources are available to him. What "pleasure and repose" or "domestic joy" await the pensive poet, who is still after all a neglected sighing shrub on a foreign mountainside? If the message that "no loud storms" need annoy the individual will be of little comfort to the exiled villager, above whom "the giddy temper flies," it will be hardly more consoling to the poet himself, elevated only temporarily "above the storm's career" on his mountain.

In effect Johnson's conclusion to the poem subverts all that has preceded, prescribing indifference not merely to the poet's own fate and "proper cares" (l. 101), but to all that had enabled him to move sympathetically out of the self: the hope of greater happiness for mankind, sorrow at the dangers of corruption in man and society, anxiety at the specific evils threatening his own country. Goldsmith's only contribution in the last ten lines is a single couplet (ll. 435–36), which revealingly alludes to two examples of barbarous and excruciating punishment of those who dared to oppose the *status quo:* in the context of Johnson's dignified and reassuring conclusion, they obtrude as if to register the painful suppression of sympathetic imagination which has taken place.

Ultimately, of course, as the dedication had made clear, the poet is a version of Oliver Goldsmith, who has after all made his way from his mountaintop to London, where he is now publishing his poem as an act of wild poetic ambition. Whatever problems the disturbed and disturbing poetic self had created within *The Traveller,* it would not seem unreasonable to conclude that one purpose of the poem was the self-dramatization of the poet; or, inverting the recent "rhetorical" approach, to assert that its philosophical and political content should be read as no more than a rhetorical device for winning respect and sympathy for the poet. Frederick M. Keener has recently described Pope as "a man who, with more dedication than any English poet before him, tried to speak out of his own quotidian life in an attempt to win the love of his readers, by being, as much as possible, convincingly himself" (*An Essay on Pope*). If Goldsmith, less adequately equipped in most ways than Pope, was similarly seeking the love of his readers, his poem apparently won it for him. Hitherto an anonymous or laughable figure in the literary world, Goldsmith was suddenly respected and celebrated. According to Sir Joshua Reynolds, "His *Traveller* produced an eagerness unparalleled to see the author. He was sought after with greediness." Mrs. Cholmondeley, after hearing the poem read aloud by Johnson, graciously exclaimed, "I never more shall think Dr. Goldsmith ugly."

III

The evidence of *The Traveller* suggests that Goldsmith's instinct was to move towards what Wordsworth would later praise in "that class of poets, the principal charm of whose writings depends upon the familiar knowledge which they convey of the personal feelings of their authors." Wordsworth was discussing Burns: "On the basis of his human character he has reared a poetic one, which with more or less distinctness presents itself to view in almost every part of . . . his most valuable verses"; and again, "Not less successfully does Burns avail himself of his own character and situation in society, to construct out of them a poetic self,—introduced as a dramatic personage." Yet it is noticeable that, when he came to publish *The Deserted Village* in 1770, Goldsmith made no attempt to give the poem any literal autobiographical status. He may have become aware in *The Traveller* of the problems and restrictions entailed in such a procedure. There was, moreover, little in his actual circumstances which might encourage him to make them the basis of a dignified poetic self, as Pope had eventually done and as Cowper, for example, in a quite different way would do early in the following decade ("My delineations of the heart are from my own experience").

The rhetorical critics, refusing to treat *The Deserted Village* as literal nostalgia for his childhood on Goldsmith's part and concentrating on the poem itself, have undoubtedly illuminated certain aspects of its method and preoccupations. Their insistence on a total distinction between Goldsmith and the "I" of the poem would no doubt be more convincing if that poetic self were clearly differentiated from the "I" of *The Traveller*. Yet, as Johnson observed, the later poem was "sometimes too much the echo" of *The Traveller,* and there is nothing to indicate that the "I" in *The Deserted Village* is not essentially the same self as had proved so appealing in the earlier poem, identified firmly as Oliver Goldsmith. The characteristics and preoccupations of the later "I" are strikingly similar to those of *The Traveller*. Indeed, if elements which had tended to remain discrete or even to conflict in *The Traveller* are now more adequately fused, it is through a more consistent and intimate presentation of the poetic self and its response to the ruined landscape in which the poet stands. The emphatic account of "my wanderings round this world of care" (ll. 83–96) and search for happiness which has brought him back to Auburn seem explicitly to allude to the poet of *The Traveller* ("My prime of life in wand'ring spent and care," l. 24), as do the themes of dispossession and exile and the tones of patriotic indignation. If both poems could be described as topographical, the landscape of Auburn is, of course, surveyed in no judicious cosmopolitan spirit: what now concerns the poet is the landscape of memory, an internalized topography. As a result, the disparity between the problematic and judicious selves in *The Traveller* is replaced by a relatively unified poetic self, whose melancholy is explicable and justified, and whose personal emotional involvement is more sustained. What had remained at best a tentative recognition in *The Traveller* of the shared fate of poet and exiled villagers becomes in *The Deserted Village* the poem's central situation.

Recent critics of the poem would still consider such features of the poem as subservient to its primary aim of persuasion to a political viewpoint (however defined). In this situation the poem's dedication turns out once more to be relevant. *The Deserted Village* is addressed to a much more distinguished figure than Henry Goldsmith, but Goldsmith noticeably makes Sir Joshua Reynolds a fraternal substitute for the brother who had died in 1768: "The only dedication I ever made was to my brother, because I loved him better than most other men. He is since dead. Permit me to inscribe this Poem to you." Goldsmith then makes what must seem a remarkable admission about his poem. He acknowledges that Reynolds, like "several of our best and wisest friends," will object that the rural depopulation it deplores does not exist and that "the disorders it laments are only to be found in the poet's own imagination." To such a reaction Goldsmith can oppose only the sincerity of his convictions and his conscientious observations in the countryside. Yet the whole question of rural depopulation, implicitly admitted to be controversial and complex, would require more elaborate discussion than he wishes to offer. He prefers not to "tire the reader with a long preface," when he wants instead "his unfatigued attention to a long poem." Goldsmith's final paragraph relates his views on depopulation to the increasing "luxury," which politicians consider to be a national advantage. Allying himself with the ancients in the belief that luxury destroys kingdoms, he admits that "so much has been poured out of late on the other side of the question" that his own views are virtually isolated.

Goldsmith surely concedes a remarkable amount, not merely to economists, politicians, and the general tide of opinion, but to the views of his "best and wisest friends," such as Reynolds. It is more than an admission that his views are highly personal, since he acknowledges that those who know him best believe that the poem really embodies the "disorders" of the poet's own imagination. Nothing in the rest of the dedication is calculated to challenge this judgment. The effect of the dedication is not, as in the case of *The Traveller*, to identify the poem as literally autobiographical, but to emphasize its direct relationship to Oliver Goldsmith in another way, in its origin in his idiosyncratic imagination.

It is hard to believe that Goldsmith was unaware of the reaction he would obtain. Indeed, his dedication may even have encouraged it. The first reviewers of *The Deserted Village* all separated what they took to be its highly dubious politicoeconomic argument from its unusual imaginative appeal. If, as we are now told, the poem's rhetorical purpose was political persuasion, it should at least be admitted that, as far as its immediate audience was concerned, the poem was a striking rhetorical failure. The first readers of *The Deserted Village* evidently thought it quite as reasonable to read the political content as an occasion for the exercise of the poet's sensibility and imagination, as to insist that these aspects of the poem were purely rhetorical in function. It is also an undeniable fact that within a generation admirers of *The Deserted Village* were assiduously exploring every possible autobiographical feature of the poem, and investigations of its literal origins in the poet's own childhood in Ireland had reached elaborate proportions by 1811. No earlier English poem had excited—or invited?—such a response.

Goldsmith's emphasis on his "imagination" in the dedication, however, may have been an instinctive precaution against a too literal reading of the poem, either as autobiography or as an economic tract. It is worth emphasizing that *The Deserted Village* is only incidentally (ll. 305–8) concerned with the enclosure and redistribution of the land, which undoubtedly had a disturbing effect on the poorer rural classes, but which was an essential accompaniment to the major agricultural improvements which took place during the century. Goldsmith's concern is primarily with a different and tangential issue, the acquisition and improvement of pleasure parks by wealthy members of the aristocracy and middle class. In certain cases the improvement of such estates could involve the clearance of local communities, although Goldsmith's friends and reviewers refused to believe that the practice was widespread. Yet out of this situation Goldsmith devised a simple formula for England's ruin, which his imagination found deeply compelling: wealth made in the colonies is being used in Britain to force the humbler rural classes to emigrate to the colonies. For this reason, Goldsmith's pessimistic vision, in a period proud of its agricultural achievements, is of a countryside in the process of devastation; and for the same reason that vision was from the first recognized as highly idiosyncratic. Even Goldsmith's own dedication concedes his friends' belief that he was reading his own problems into the landscape.

As for the poetic self within *The Deserted Village,* in spite of efforts to reduce it to pastoral, georgic, or loco-descriptive conventions, there is no precedent, except less elaborately in Gray's *Elegy,* for a poem in which the poet's own memory and imagination actively recreate its essential landscape. John Scott of Amwell, in the long discussion of the poem in his *Critical Essays* (1785), was puzzled by its "desultory structure" (apparently failing to recognize its artful rhetorical design as expounded by recent critics). Yet Scott's desire for a more orderly contrast between Auburn in the past and in the present might in itself point to what Goldsmith was in fact attempting: a structure which went some way to embody the flux of personal emotion and memory, the coexistence of past and present in the reflecting mind.

To state as much is merely to make clear the obvious psychological and poetic limits to Goldsmith's ability or intention to render with "Romantic" fidelity the subtle movements of consciousness. *The Deserted Village* is very far from being mere emotional flux. The repeated contrasts of the once happy and now deserted village lead to indignant general conclusions about the reasons for this state of affairs. Goldsmith's manner is at times didactic and oratorical. "Sweet Auburn" *is* an idealized embodiment of health, innocence, and contentment, and of doomed rural virtues in general. The poet, although affectionately remembering the "seats of my youth," tends to remain an observer of the village's life even in his recollections, loitering and pausing in the landscape, hearing Auburn's mingled sounds from a hillside, ultimately detached as if in part the reader's sympathetic representative in his own memories, with touches of self-conscious condescension at times to the "honest rustics." On the other hand, his account of his hopes of returning to Auburn to impress the villagers with his knowledge of the world is disarmingly derisive of this very role (ll. 89–90), and his personal response to Auburn is most convincing when simplest and most specific, as in the description of its evening sounds and in the central character sketches. John Scott's comments on the diction of such passages can remind us of the original freshness of what we now take for granted. Such passages seemed to Scott to "convey village ideas, in village language" and only just to escape being "prosaick or mean": they are acceptable only "because we know that they are the effect of choice, not of incapacity."

Scott also drew attention, with some distaste, to another aspect of the poem's diction, which may lead finally to preoccupations in the poem ignored in recent discussions. As Scott pointed out, certain words are repeated, especially in the opening description of Auburn, in an almost obsessive manner: "sweet," "lovely," "smiling," "dear," "charms." Goldsmith's aim seems not merely to have been to achieve an almost incantatory lyrical effect at points (for example, ll. 31–36), but to insist by means of this diction on the sexual identity of Auburn as an innocent girl, who will be betrayed, raped, or prostituted. The "bashful virgin" (l. 29), and "coy maid" (l. 249), who help to focus this aspect of the happy village before the outrageous activities of the "tyrant" (l. 37) (the exact nature of his desecration is left vague at first), are survived in the ruined village only by the "wretched matron," "yon widowed, solitary thing" (ll. 129–136), who must laboriously eke out a pathetic living from the wasteland. She is not, of course, quite the sole survivor, for she has been joined by the poet himself. In a way that at first seems only incidentally curious, the poet and the wretched old woman are equated by the description of her as "The sad historian of the pensive plain" (l. 136).

The sexual theme becomes explicit in lines 287–302, the repetitions of "charm" and "charms" linking the passage with the opening description of Auburn. Goldsmith compares a declining nation, betrayed by luxury and resorting to surprising splendors while its peasants are scourged from the land, to a "fair female," who could afford to be "unadorned and plain" in her youthful beauty, owing nothing to art, but who must resort to "all the glaring impotence of dress" as her "frail" charms fade. Auburn itself had embodied the health and innocent condition of the nation, yet the "fair female['s]" vulnerability to the processes of time in Goldsmith's simile might seem to give the nation's decline an inevitability distinct from the specific causes he deplores. Underlying the passage is that familiar and virtually irresistible cycle from simplicity to refinement to decadence which animates so much of Goldsmith's writing about politics, history, and the arts.

Almost immediately the sexual theme recurs, as the poet sympathetically imagines the fate of villagers driven to the city. Such exiles include "the poor houseless shivering female," lying "near her betrayer's door" (ll. 325–36). Yet unexpectedly, Goldsmith makes clear that it was this girl's own ambition, not the depredations of the "tyrant," which had led her to leave her innocent village for the town. Such an emphasis might suggest a vulnerability in Auburn itself (not merely to time or to the local "tyrant") hardly to Goldsmith's purpose, although the "frail" charms of the female in the earlier simile (l. 291) might now retrospectively acquire a further sexual

implication. Goldsmith, however, explicitly refuses to envisage a similar fate
for the "fair tribes" of Auburn, who are obliged to emigrate instead (ll.
337–41). Yet the description of the ruined girl may have implications which
go beyond incidental pathos. Within the poem only one other ambitious
wanderer had voluntarily left the country for the town, the poet himself,
and the possibility emerges that his fate, involving some loss of innocence or
prostitution of his talents, has been similar.

Throughout the poem the obtrusion of the poet's own memories, hopes,
and disappointments have entangled his experience inextricably with that of
Auburn. Its innocence had been his, its destruction the ruin of his hopes, and
the sympathy the villagers deserve is hardly to be distinguished from the
sympathy to which the poet himself is entitled. In Gray's *Elegy* the escape
from the predicament of the mournful poetic self is enacted by means of
sympathy for others (villagers once more), which in turn entitles the poet to
a sympathetic epitaph: the poet, inhibited from demanding sympathy directly on his own behalf, can arouse it for a projection of the deprived self.
The same process is enacted in different terms and with less inhibition in
The Deserted Village. As in *The Traveller,* the villagers are exiled to a
strange and menacing environment. By now, they have become little more
than personifications of the rural virtues whose supposed disappearance the
poet deplores (l. 363ff.).

The effect of this disembodiment of the villagers is to allow a final
emphatic obtrusion in the poem by the poet himself, which has perplexed
some critics but which serves to bring to the surface a number of underlying
preoccupations. The poet, pondering in the ruined landscape on the departure of the "rural virtues" from England, unexpectedly reveals in his long
final apostrophe that "sweet Poetry" is also departing:

> And thou, sweet Poetry, thou loveliest maid,
> Still first to fly where sensual joys invade;
> Unfit in these degenerate times of shame,
> To catch the heart, or strike for honest fame;
> Dear charming nymph, neglected and decried,
> My shame in crowds, my solitary pride.
> Thou source of all my bliss, and all my woe,
> That found'st me poor at first, and keep'st me so.
>   (ll. 407–14)

This is no mere routine assertion of the link between poetry and liberty.
It would appear that poetry itself and the poet's renunciation of her—or,
perhaps, poetry's renunciation of the poet—rather than politics or econom-

ics is the true subject of the poem. The reappearance of the recurrent diction of its opening links "sweet Poetry," "loveliest maid," "Dear charming nymph" with sweet, lovely, dear, charming Auburn in its happiness; and poetry can preserve her virtue from "sensual joys"—rape and prostitution—only by departure and exile. Auburn evidently represented not merely the rural virtues which avarice destroys, but the kind of poetry which is rooted in them and which is similarly vulnerable in a commercial society. Poetry's inability "To catch the heart, or strike for honest fame" recalls precisely Goldsmith's pessimism, in his dedication to *The Traveller,* about the folly of poetical ambition and the poet's inability to reach the heart. In a society where poetry is "neglected and decried," it becomes a furtive, introspective pursuit, "My shame in crowds, my solitary pride." The poet's poverty, a favorite topic of Goldsmith, is only an outward manifestation of the indifference of society to his art. A less clearly articulated consequence of the female personification of poetry is the suggestion in lines 411–14 of some inadequacy in the poet himself, as if poetry were a beautiful woman whom the poet had compromised and could not honestly maintain. Having come close to a personal renunciation of his art (at least one reviewer reading the passage so), Goldsmith depersonalizes the final lines, encouraging poetry to resume her proper role elsewhere than in Britain, notably in remote and primitive parts of the world. Samuel Johnson once more stepped in to close down the poem, with four massively clinching lines (ll. 427–30).

Thus *The Deserted Village* itself enacts the collapse of the very poetic conventions in which it might have sought refuge: the pastoral and georgic modes are devastated within the poet's own imagination, the traditional celebration of retirement (ll. 97–112) is mocked by the ruined village to which the poet has "retired," the only topography worth describing is the landscape of memory, the tyrant's ravages are a hideous parody of the tradition of "country house" poetry still available to Pope, and the whole poem negates the familiar "Whig" panegyric of English commerce and liberty.

The closing lines of the poem finally (in more than one sense) invoke another poetic form, the "progress poem," in which Augustan poets had celebrated the westward migration of poetry and liberty from ancient Greece to Britain. It is possible, however, to overestimate the optimism implicit in the form. As Aubrey Williams has shown, *The Dunciad* is in one aspect a grotesque inversion of the process, describing instead the relentless progress of barbarism and darkness; and even if such poets as Collins and Gray had continued to explore the form, an increasingly frustrated note of uncertainty about the actual "progress" of poetry and liberty in Britain is evident.

Goldsmith's variation of the form is drastic in its implications. The closing lines of *The Deserted Village* apparently dramatize that precise moment in the "progress" of poetry when she necessarily departs from Britain's shores in search of a more hospitable environment. As she does so, Goldsmith is driven to counter his own despair by uncharacteristically apostrophising the primitive visionary role of poetry, its connections with liberty and prophecy, the functions it can no longer perform in England. He does so partly by echoing the lines in Gray's *The Progress of Poesy* which describe, in the words of Gray's note, the "Extensive influence of poetic Genius over the remotest and most uncivilised nations; its connection with liberty, and the virtues that naturally attend on it." Unlike Collins and Gray, who had sought ways of availing themselves of it in their own poetry, Goldsmith could only acknowledge this power and then renounce it, envisaging no personal compensation or redemption in the visionary powers of the imagination. Left alone in a landscape which is at once "a garden, and a grave" (l. 302), he has no role but the provision of appropriate epitaphs for those who survive only in his memory, and for his own art. His poem has enacted what, a decade earlier, he had dreaded: that "the muse shall seldom be heard, except in plaintive elegy, as if she wept her own decline."

JAMES H. LEHMANN

The Vicar of Wakefield:
Goldsmith's Sublime, Oriental Job

The breakdown of typological exegesis in the eighteenth century in England and Germany, which has been documented fully in Hans Frei's *The Eclipse of Biblical Narrative,* was accompanied by two crucial developments in the history of Scriptural reading. The first was the *Orientalizing* of the Bible, that is, the reading of it as a product and reflection of an Oriental and therefore of a primitive society. The second involves reading the Scriptures as expressive writing, more specifically as *sublime* poetry. This double transformation is entirely consistent with the dissolution of the old typological framework. For if the Old Testament no longer *means* the New Testament (and that, as Frei argues, is essentially what typology is all about), then it must mean something else. And so its old spiritual referent (the "prefigured" New Testament) is replaced by its geographical and historical referent (the "Orient") and by its emotional and poetic referent (the sublime soul of the ancient Hebrew poet).

These three moments in the history of exegesis—the breakdown in typological reading, the growth of an Orientalizing mode in biblical criticism, and the discovery of the sublime in the Hebrew Scripture—were all fundamentally *secularizing* moments. Taken as a cultural complex, they constitute a prime example of what Kenneth Burke has called a "secular conversion." Burke's term denotes those attempts by the human mind to neutralize the sacred and terrible by *renaming* them and thus making them more manageable. The Bible, in this sense, was *renamed* "Oriental" and

From *ELH* 46, no. 1 (Spring 1979). © 1979 by The Johns Hopkins University Press, Baltimore/London.

"sublime" as a way of deflecting its theological force. That recourse to the sublime is generally a strategy of avoidance has been noted by Geoffrey Hartman, who claims that the sublime is always a form of sublimation. For our purposes it is sufficient to recall that, as Thomas Weiskel writes in *The Romantic Sublime*, "in the history of literary consciousness the sublime revives as God withdraws from an immediate participation in the experience of men."

It is true that the English critical tradition had long referred to the Hebrew Bible as uniquely sublime, often as a way of excusing its apparent violation of canons of poetic diction. But Robert Lowth, in his Oxford lectures delivered from 1741 to 1750 and published in 1753 as *De Sacra Poesi Hebraeorum,* was the first to combine the claim of biblical sublimity with a detailed treatment of the poetry as Oriental literature. He argued that an understanding of the Bible presupposed an appreciation of the character of the Hebrew "Orientals" to whom it was addressed and by whom it was written. The natural imagery contained in this poetry must be ascribed to the natural surroundings of the ancient Hebrews such as might be reconstructed from modern travelers' reports of Arabia. The sublimity of the Hebrew is related, for Lowth, to the rude origins of the poetry: the didacticism of the poetry, what Lowth calls its "sententiousness," was "more likely to prove efficacious with men in a rude stage of society, for it professed not to dispute but to command, not persuade but to compel." The Oriental quality of the Hebrew mind similarly would make it unable to develop abstract concepts such as that of a future world.

The Oriental quality of the Hebrew mind, its concreteness, its closeness to nature and to the natural context out of which it arose, is closely linked by Lowth to the sublime language of passion that distinguishes Hebrew writing from all others: "The language of Reason is cool, temperate, rather humble than elevated, well arranged and perspicuous, with an evident care and anxiety lest anything should escape which might appear perplexed or obscure. The language of the Passions is totally different: the conceptions burst out in a turbid stream, expressive in a manner of the internal conflict; the more vehement break out in hasty confusion; they catch (without search or study) whatever is impetuous, vivid or energetic. In a word, Reason speaks literally, the Passions poetically." The Rabbis, therefore, must have erred when they declared that prophecy proceeds only from an untroubled mind: "On the contrary, we learn from the testimony of the Prophets themselves that the art of prophesying was often if not always accompanied with a very violent agitation of the mind."

Lowth's use of the sublime as a means of biblical analysis is a *secular* substitute for the earlier spiritual readings of the Old Testament. Significantly, Lowth's lectures generally stay clear of matters Christological, "mystical and visionary." Instead he focuses on the use of parallelism as a rhetorical device in Hebrew verse, and on a theory of parabolic language that permits expression of the sublime through the periodic verse of the Hebrew Bible. He is much less interested in explicating spiritual meanings than in describing the sublime in the Psalms or Isaiah.

Lowth's influence was widespread. M. H. Abrams ascribes particular importance to Lowth: on the mirror/lamp continuum he is something of a proto-lamp. Lowth's notion of the sublime poetic imitation of the poet's soul therefore marks a shift from a more external idea of natural imitation in the Augustan Age (*The Mirror and the Lamp: Romantic Theory and the Critical Tradition*). His work was known and admired by Christopher Smart, whose ecstatic verse utilized Lowthian parallelisms. Hugh Blair's defense of Ossian (1763) rested in large part on the "sublimity" Ossian shared with the Hebrew Bible. Sir William Jones's *Asiatick Researches* (1772) shows an equal debt to the *Lectures on the Sacred Poetry of the Hebrews*. Three years after its first edition, Lowth's *Lectures* were enthusiastically received by Johann David Michaelis, the greatest German Bible scholar of his day. Michaelis's annotations of the *Lectures* (Göttingen, 1758, and Oxford, 1763) led to its wide dissemination in Europe. Finally, Lowth motivated Herder's key work, *Vom Geist der ebräischen Poesie* (1782). Even this cursory history of Lowth's reception would indicate the sentimental and literary possibilities implicit in his new approach to a sublime, Oriental Scriptures: the Sacred Text is sublimely expressive because it is Oriental; it is Oriental because it is so expressive. That these two notions were seen as adequate explanations for Old Testament poetry shows that there was a decided shift away from finding univocal spiritual meanings in the Bible, and instead toward considering the language of the text as a vehicle of poetic expression.

The "sublime" was one secular aspect of Orientalism. Another manifestation of the "secular conversion" I see in biblical Orientalism was the growing prominence of comparative Semitic philology. In a sense what was being undertaken by mid-century Semiticists was nothing less than the demythologizing of Hebrew as the Sacred Tongue. As Arabic and Syriac came to be more widely studied, Hebrew lost its privileged position. The claim that Hebrew was not the oldest Semitic language, indeed that it was linguistically poorer than Arabic or Syriac, was made during the 1730s by [Albrecht] Schultens. Not coincidentally, it was Schultens who first proposed the notion of "Semitic languages." The utility of the notion of a comparative Semitics is obvious: if one is going to *rename* (in Burke's sense) the Bible as Oriental literature, then it is important that there be a "related" body to which one may assimilate it.

Crucially, it is the Book of Job that first became the focus for the Orientalizing Bible critics of the eighteenth century. It is this book that was first de-Hebraized by these critics, and so detached from the sacred history of the Jewish and Christian traditions. As long ago as the times of the Talmud, the Rabbis had already sensed something very unbiblical about this book. There never was any consensus regarding its authorship or date of composition. Schultens proposed that the work was not of Jewish origin (a possibility entertained by the rabbis of the Talmud). Some scholars suggested that Job was written in Arabic and then translated into Hebrew.

Dropping Job from the history of the Israelites had obvious theological implications for eighteenth-century students of the Bible. This was remarked over a century ago by the German Hebraist Franz Delitzsch, who noted that:

> With the commentary of Albert Schultens . . . a new epoch in the exposition [of Job] begins. He was the first to bring the Semitic languages, and chiefly the Arabic, to bear on the translation and rightly so, for . . . Jerome in his preface to Daniel had before correctly remarked *Iob cum arabica lingua plurimam habet societatem*. Reiske (1779) and Schnurrer (1781) followed later in the footsteps of Schultens but *in proportion as the Israelitish element was considered in connection with the Oriental, the divine distinctiveness of the former was forgotten* [emphasis added].

Lowth, too, saw Job as a non-Jewish work. He believed that although written *in* Hebrew, it was not written *by* a Hebrew, but rather by an Idumean writing somewhere east of Palestine. Although in his novel treatments of Isaiah and the Psalms Lowth at times speaks of spiritual meanings (however halfheartedly), in the case of Job he explicitly and emphatically rejects what he derides as "mystical allegory." The Book of Job has nothing to do, he says, with the religion of the Israelites. Lowth "is not able to trace any vestige of an allegorical meaning throughout the entire poem." For him the central lesson of Job is in no way doctrinal; he scoffs at the numerous allegorical readings and spiritual meanings ascribed to the work. "The truth of the narrative would never . . . have been called into question, but from the immoderate affection of some allegorizing mystics for their own fictions which run to such excess as to prevent them from acceding to anything but what was visionary and typical." Lowth rejects doctrinal readings as utterly irrelevant to "this extraordinary monument of ancient wisdom."

Job is uniquely sublime for Lowth, as it is uniquely Oriental: "The dignity of the style is answerable to that of the subject, its force and energy to the greatness of those passions which it describes, and as this production excels all the other remains of the Hebrew Poetry in economy and arrangement, so it yields to none in sublimity of style." Job is the most sublime of Hebrew works, the most ancient, the most primitive, and the least theological. It is the most clearly Oriental and "has no relation whatever to the affairs of the Israelites."

If Job then is not a doctrinal work for Lowth, it is nevertheless a work containing a profound moral lesson. But that lesson concerns only the sublimity of its poetry as it reflects the sublime passion of its poet-hero, Job. The only doctrine here is the secular doctrine of sublime humility as expressed in the poetry of the work.

Lowth makes this radical point by distinguishing two literary structures in the Book. One, he notes, is the narrative as a whole, embodying the story of Job, his fall from fortune, and his subsequent restoration. The clear message of this biblical *narrative*, viewed as such, is patience: Job's persistence in his faith leads ultimately to his just reward. Lowth prefers to read the work as poetry, however, rather than as narrative. What Lowth calls the *poem* of Job excludes the prose prologue and epilogue of the book (which contain the fall and restoration) and deals only with its poetry. Viewed this way, as poetry unrelated to narrative action, the point of the book must be something quite different from patience. This Lowth specifies as *humility*. "The true object of the Poem [is] to demonstrate the necessity of humility, of trust in God." Viewed not as narrative but as a poem, the Book of Job points not to doctrine but to the sublime sentiments of its hero. "The Poem of Job" contains:

> No plot or action whatever, not even of the most simple kind . . .
> it contains merely a representation of those manners, passions
> and sentiments which might actually be expected in such a sit-
> uation. . . . The poem contains a great variety of sentiment . . .
> manners and character, remarkable efforts of passion, but no
> change of fortune, no plot or action.

Since the essence of the poem is the depiction of sublime passions, the characterization of Job's friends is necessarily incomplete: "There appears . . . but little difference in the manners of the three friends; *for in them the Poet has rather studied to display the progress of the passions, than any diversity of character"* [emphasis added]. Questions of Divine Providence are not to the point of this most sublime and ancient Oriental poetry: "Neither the nature nor the object of the Poem required a defense of the Divine Providence but merely a reprehension of the overconfidence of Job."

Lowth clearly points the distinction between the *narrative* of Job and the *poem* of Job. His preference for the latter is due not only to the poetic bias of the *Lectures* but also to Lowth's evident impatience with contemporary doctrinal controversies surrounding Job. By emphasizing the poem of Job, Lowth emphasizes the sublime character, whose essential quality is finally sublime humility before God's ineffable power.

II

Lowth on Job is of paramount interest when we consider the possibility of understanding the Vicar as a Job-figure in any "doctrinal" sense. The most sophisticated such view is that of Martin C. Battestin's *The Providence of Wit*. In the chapter entitled "Goldsmith: The Comedy of Job," Battestin confronts a problem that has vexed critics of this novel for some time, namely, the abrupt shift of tone and action that occurs midway through the book. Once Charles Primrose leaves his family to retrieve the abducted Olivia, we move from the story of a family to the pilgrimage of an individual, from a controlled comedy of manners with controlled narrator to a rambling tale, often interrupted by other tales, in which sentiment and pathos dominate. One approach to this structural problem has been to treat the first half of the book as novelistic success, while viewing the second half as a sort of failure in its succumbing to the use of romance motifs. Another approach to this problem has been to join the two halves thematically, and Battestin's essay attempts such a solution. He seeks to show that the story of Dr. Primrose in both halves of the novel is the story of the biblical Job. The analogy itself, Battestin admits, is not new. What is new in his treatment is the way he specifies the theological meaning of the Job-analogy. In this reading, the hero of the novel follows the path of the biblical Job in the sense that he learns the lesson, which, according to Battestin, was the common reading of Job in the period of *The Vicar's* composition. This lesson is the doctrine of equal providence, the belief "that, although the dealings of Providence are unequal in this life, the sufferings of good men will be abundantly recompensed in the hereafter." According to Battestin, Primrose learns this Christian "doctrine of futurity" in chapter 28 and shows his new wisdom in chapter 29 by preaching to his fellow prisoners on just this subject. In fact, the title of the latter chapter makes reference to the "equal dealings of Providence."

Primrose's doctrinal revelation marks his attainment of true knowledge. The theological term for Job's new knowledge, Battestin tells us, is "prudence." Whereas one might have knowledge (and Job had knowledge) he might still lack *prudence,* the insight that God's justice persists despite its apparent abrogation in this world. Battestin supports his reading by citing a large number of contemporary theologians who wrote on Job, and by citing, too, a particular controversy which raged around Warburton and Bishop Thomas Sherlock during the middle decades of the century. He suggests that Goldsmith sided with the anti-Warburtonians, who maintained that a message of divine reward in resurrection ("equal providence") could be derived from the Book of Job (and hence from a work written before the Christian dispensation).

Battestin's reading is an explicit rejection of recent attempts to read Goldsmith as ironic in his presentation of the hero. Because these readings do not take the theological context into account, he argues, they are anachronistic sophistications imposed on the text by modern critics.

Now Battestin is certainly right in drawing attention to the exegetical tradition in his analysis of *The Vicar of Wakefield.* But it is not at all clear that the Job-analogy in the novel is meant to be taken in the spirit he suggests. In fact, Goldsmith plays a good deal with the biblical story; the biblical paradigm is often invoked only to be toyed with. This is so, as my survey of Lowth might have suggested, precisely because the exegetical tradition was itself undergoing a significant change during this period.

As a preliminary but significant example of the ways Goldsmith plays with his biblical model, consider the term "prudence." Battestin wants this term to bear a great weight because it is the technical name of Job's insight; moreover, it is the term which for Battestin ties together the unifying motifs of disguise and blindness (noted [elsewhere] by Curtis Dahl) and the theological understanding of divine providence. The trouble here is that prudence is an ambiguous term in *The Vicar.* Although Battestin refers to prudence only as a term of theological art, its other uses cannot be overlooked in attempting to discern the total meaning of the word in the text. Thus, in the opening chapter, Mr. Wilmot is said to have only prudence left at the age of seventy-two. There is nothing theological about this jesting use of the word. Nor is the term used doctrinally when Primrose tells his family that no prudence could have prevented their misfortune. Actually, prudence would have consisted in Primrose's silence about his Whistonian beliefs on strict clerical monogamy until *after* his family had been joined to the wealthy

Wilmots (exactly what the messenger bearing news of the vicar's loss suggests). Prudence may well have theological connotations, but that would only make its use ironic, and irony is finally what Battestin cannot permit.

There are other reversals of the biblical types as well. Job's wife has become the biblical Deborah, the female judge, ruling Israel and ruling, too, her passive nominal leader Barak (Judges 4, 5). And as in Judges, this Deborah is always described in military terms: she is the one who conducts sieges and plans battles. Moses, the son, is something of a lawgiver: he always cites the ancients and argues weakly with Thornhill on matters of doctrine. His sententiousness, in short, is a parody of his biblical namesake and type. And then there are the crucial changes in the order of the biblical narrative, as when Deborah Primrose reprimands her husband for cursing his oppressor whereas Job's wife was the one who begged him to curse God and die. Like Parson Adams of *Joseph Andrews* (the *locus classicus* for Battestin's method), our Vicar often acts at variance with his prototype, deviating subtly but surely from his presumed prefiguration.

There are many such deviations in *The Vicar of Wakefield,* but my purpose is not so much to list them as to indicate where Battestin has gone wrong in his general approach. Battestin's fundamental error arises from his assumption that the *analogical* structure persists in Goldsmith's fiction. Battestin has totally ignored the fact that from the 1740s onward new ways of reading the Bible were gaining ground in England and that such changes in reading would have suggested a number of possible alternatives for the application of a scriptural text to a literary work. He does not consider that the way (a reader of) Pope would have read his Bible might differ from the way (a reader of) Goldsmith would have read the Bible. For example, Pope in his use of Balaam and Job in the *Epistle to Bathurst* (1733) assumes a definite series of theological connotations attached to those figures that can be read as constituting their *meaning;* Earl Wasserman's analysis of the *Epistle* was based on just this premise. But a quarter century later the Bible was being read differently; it was seen not only as the vehicle for theological meanings, but also as a repository of sublime poetry in the Oriental mode. Battestin must be aware of this new Orientalized Bible, yet he pays no attention to it. The results of his exhaustive researches into the theological literature are thus prejudiced by his implicit decision to consider only the homiletic aspects of these writings and to ignore the grammatical and literary-critical work on the Bible that was flourishing at just this time.

Battestin's homiletic bias in this regard forces him also to assume that it was the Warburtonian controversy on "equal providence" that stimulated interest in the Book of Job. Thus, after listing the commentators ranged on each side, he writes, "in the same period appeared several other, more or less neutral, treatises reflecting the widespread interest in the subject which the controversy had generated. These include a variety of studies by Daniel Bellamy, William Worthington, Walter Hodge, Leonard Chappelow, Thomas Heath and Bishop Lowth." The unexamined assumption that these "neutral" studies merely reflect the theological controversy leads Battestin to ignore the new Orientalizing of the Bible undertaken by just these "more or less neutral studies." It also leads him to ignore the fictional possibilities which a newly Orientalized Bible might present to writers such as Goldsmith.

Battestin's evidence of Goldsmith's purportedly sincere interest in the controversy also deserves scrutiny. This consists of a review of Hawkins' contribution to the debate that appeared in the *Critical Review* of August 1759. Its authorship by Goldsmith is uncertain, but in any case the following hardly reveals real interest in the affair:

> Mr. Hawkins seems to be pretty confident in the advantage of his cause; and this we may venture to say, that he seems to be on the safe side, for he is on the bishop's; and though he loses his cause he may gain a vicarage. As for the controversy, so much has been said on both sides, that we must really acknowledge ourselves sceptic in the debate. . . . We can know enough and believe enough without being acquainted with a syllable of the matter: we could wish our divines would therefore rather turn their arms against the common enemy; and while infidelity is at the gate, not waste their time in civil altercation.

This passage is clearly not the strongest basis upon which to found Goldsmith's interest in the Providential controversies surrounding the Book of Job. Rather, in Goldsmith as in other Job studies, the general indifference to the theological issues that Battestin holds most important suggests that he has ignored a crucial development in the mid-century reading of Job. Far from there being a consensus with regard to the specific theology of the work, there was not even unanimity as to whether the book was to be taken as *primarily* theological.

The new Orientalizing Bible readings, as exemplified by Lowth, are important therefore because they force us to reconsider the historical plausibility of a strictly theological reading of Job in *The Vicar of Wakefield*. What we have instead is a *secular* Job. Ronald Paulson has elaborated the distinction between *emblem* and *expression* in the art and literature of the eighteenth century. We might apply this notion by noting that in the

Orientalist tradition represented by Bishop Lowth, the emblematic quality
of Scripture is confronted with the expressive potentialities of Hebrew poetry. For a new tradition of Biblical Orientalism, the emblematic readability
of the Bible (the old typological framework in which the Old Testament is
emblematic of the New) has been transformed into its sublime expressive-
ness. Scripture no longer *means* the way it once did. This "secular conversion" is never more manifest than in the Orientalizing of the Book of Job.

III

I would suggest that there is a moral development in *The Vicar* that is
closely related to a movement toward the attainment of the sublime. This
movement takes our Job-figure from an essentially ironic condition to one
that sublimely transcends irony through love and humility. Primrose *becomes* a Job-figure in the course of the novel, not because he acquires
specific theological knowledge, but because he moves beyond an artificially
self-conscious situation into the condition of genuine passion. He attains the
sublime when he is motivated not by concern for appearances and social
status, but by the natural and passionate love of his family and his fellow
man.

This moral movement in the novel towards humility and the sublime
can best be seen in the progress of the work's pictorial imagery. In Goldsmith's time sublime painting, like sublime Hebrew poetry, had to be
uniquely expressive, not emblematic. As Reynolds put it, painting must
strike its viewer in a single blow.

Both halves of our novel contain many scenes with a strongly pictorial
quality, but Goldsmith depicts these scenes differently in the two halves. In
the "pre-exilic" first portion of the work Primrose's presentation of these
pictorial scenes is intensely ironic. This is because his concern in represent-
ing his family is to curry favor with his social betters. This concern is
morally flawed; in terms of the sublime work of art, Primrose's act of
representation is mere parody. Once the vicar sets off on his journey, however, he becomes the object of forces beyond his control. Primrose no longer
creates scenes; these are discovered or reveal themselves to him. It is just this
powerlessness, and the recognition of powerlessness, that allows the narrator to transcend the irony that marks his earlier artifice. The frozen order of
the earlier depictions gives way to a series of passionate events. Our hero
recognizes moral truth just when these events convey not the ironic fiction-
making of their author, but rather his perception of the overpowering significance of human love. As he loses control over his surroundings, he gains

his ultimate redemption as a simple and sublime Job (and simplicity is an integral element of the biblical and artistic sublime). Especially in the pictorial culmination of each half of the book—the portrait scene in chapter 16 and the prison scene in chapter 29—we can contrast the irony of artifice with the simplicity of the sublime.

I am suggesting, then, that the identification of Job with the sublime in contemporary biblical discourse allows us to re-evaluate the evident break in the style of the novel. While we seem to be moving (unhappily) from a delicate novelistic depiction of life as a social environment, to life as a journey, we were in fact advancing from an artificial and unnatural mode of self-realization to a wiser vision of human existence. I would suggest, too, that a useful general notion for dealing with this transformation of pictorial imagery is that of the *frame*. This notion subsumes, in the first place, the general symbolism of spatial enclosure: frames, enclosures of all sorts, are a fundamental structure in the novel. In addition, we can talk of the *activity* of framing as it pertains to our hero-narrator. In this second sense, framing denotes a selection, delimitation, and depiction of reality by means of the imagery of enclosure. To the extent that scenes in our novel are fictionally enclosed and distanced, successive framings can be seen as the vehicles of Goldsmith's moral statement: if the activity of framing by the hero-narrator consists in the self-conscious wrenching of reality from its human context in order to re-present it (as it does, I believe, in the first half of the novel), then it is a fundamentally ironic activity. When, however, frames disclose a dominant concern for the human and the passionate, then they partake of the sublime. To return to the terminology of contemporary art criticism we might say that the sublime draws us away from the external accentuation of circumstances into the passionate center. Thus the sublime is attained only when the frame encloses that which strikes at a single blow, when the frame yields its own independent significance to the expressive force of its content. In the case of *The Vicar* ironic frames are those created by Primrose as narrator out of concern for external circumstances, social vanity, and acceptance by his social betters. Sublime frames, on the other hand, are those images of enclosure that reveal the passion of true human relationships based on love. Primrose does not create *these* scenes; they effectively create *him* and reshape his character as a sublime Job-figure. As we follow the transformation of frames in *The Vicar of Wakefield*, we follow the progress of a Job-figure transcending irony by assuming the role of sublime character.

The first half of *The Vicar* is replete with examples of framing, but none partakes of the characteristics of the biblical sublime. The women spend their time watching themselves in mirrors. When they move to a new apartment, the narrator describes the new dwelling as if he were showing us a painting ("The eye was agreeably relieved"). We are shown, through the many descriptions of the family's neat little enclosures, the pictorial and fundamentally external quality of their existence. The vicar himself is strongly implicated in this arranging process, and this despite his early assertion that "mere outside is so very trifling a circumstance with me." He speaks of his family as a republic to which he gives laws, but these laws, as he tells us, are entirely ceremonial. This needless form of social creation, which is obviously no more than ornament, is thematically set against a similar scene in a different setting, the prison, in which Primrose does indeed establish a form of useful republic among the prisoners. At the Thornhill estate, however, frames are concerned with external circumstances and, hence, are ultimately ironic.

We have a sense in the novel, also, of the fragility of these self-conscious frames that reflects the precarious social situation of the family. This is emphasized at the beginning of chapter 5 when the pastoral setting in which the Primroses are framed by the narrator is suddenly intruded upon by the hunting squire. The sense of violent intrusion into an enclosed family circle is equally apparent when the Misses Skeggs and Blarney enter in chapter 11. One detects in these scenes the vulnerability of the family circle to the reality that surrounds it, but also the ironic vulnerability of the narrator (the creator of the circle) in his eagerness to appease those powers that surround him. The vicar's language in the course of chapter 11 conveys perfectly the moral ambiguities of concern for the "mere outside"; the concern for the external sets in motion the need to accommodate oneself to the outside. That is what Primrose is doing in this chapter and that is what he does—as hero and as narrator—throughout the first half of the book.

The multiplying ironies in the first half at *The Vicar* should bring us back to the matter of Job. Powerlessness, after all, is the fundamental characteristic of Job in the Bible, and it is Primrose's lack of power that is being pointed out here. Given the general paradigm of Job, there is a pervasive irony underlying the early happy chapters. For Job has already fallen (i.e., lost his wealth) but life goes on. The anguished debate that followed immediately upon the biblical Job's fall has been transformed into the hour and a half set aside daily by the vicar "for innocent mirth between my wife and daughter in philosophical arguments between my son and me," or into the facetious debates between Thornhill and Moses on religious doctrine, or into Olivia's great skill in debating which, according to her proud mother, she has attained from reading the debates of Square and Thwackum, and of

Robinson Crusoe and Friday. Clearly, the Job pattern is being parodied precisely to highlight the artificiality of the Primroses' existence.

It is during another framed scene that a simpler, more natural, and more sublime taste is first expressed by the virtuous Burchell. Our narrator describes his discussion of the virtues of the various poetic forms with Moses and the humble Burchell. "Two blackbirds answered each other from opposite hedges . . . every sound seemed but the echo of tranquility." Within this verbally painted enclosure, the disguised lord sings the ballad of Edwin and Angelina. A moment earlier he had attacked the artificiality of the modern classicizing taste in poetry (a taste that had been defended by Moses, who always defends the ancients). The simple and the sublime, of course, were closely identified by contemporary theorists (and especially by apologists for the Bible's style). Burchell's choice of the ballad form and his pronouncements on art introduce an important theme in the novel, and are a key to the new and different structure of its second half.

The artifice of framing and the irony of posturing are most clearly opposed to Goldsmith's ideal of the natural, the simple, and the sublime in chapters 15 and 16. At the end of chapter 15, after the vicar has misconstrued Burchell's letter, he and Deborah confront the disguised Sir William. Primrose cites Pope's line in praise of the honest man. To "the hackney'd maxim of Pope," Burchell responds, "we might as well prefer the tame correct paintings of the Flemish school to the erroneous but sublime animation of the Roman pencil." Burchell rejects the correct in favor of the sublime (this dichotomy had often been applied to the Bible). In a 1760 review of Kedington's *Critical Dissertations upon the Iliad of Homer,* Goldsmith had written:

> The merit of every work is determined not from the number of its faults but of its beauties. . . . The great beauties of every work make it inestimable; its defects are only arguments of humanity, not weakness.

For this reason, Goldsmith expresses a preference for the beauties of Italian painting over the more correct French style. Goldsmith on painting and Burchell on Pope should be considered in light of the Advertisement introducing *The Vicar of Wakefield:*

> There are a hundred faults in this thing, and a hundred things might be said to prove them beauties. But it is needless. A book may be amusing with numerous errors, or it may be very dull without a single absurdity.

Opposed to this stands the ridiculous Primrose family portrait, in whose execution the vicar plays no small part. "The family use art which is opposed with still Greater" is the punning title of chapter 16. Literally, it refers to Deborah's schemes to ensnare the young Thornhill, which the narrator knows to be hopeless. But it also echoes the portrait scene in which, to outdo the Flamboroughs, as the vicar approvingly tells us, the family has been artistically represented in a single large frame. The artificiality of this framing is emphasized by the absurdity of the poses: Deborah is Venus surrounded by cupids, and Charles Primrose is depicted handing his sermons on clerical monogamy to his Venus-wife. The painter is asked to fill in "as many sheep as he could for nothing," merely to populate this contrived, unnatural space. The resulting picture, a monstrous caricature of life, won't fit in the house (another, more natural, frame) and we are told that it remained in the kitchen, a monument, it would seem, to the folly and impossibility of the whole enterprise. Coming as it does immediately after the break with Burchell and the latter's discourse on art, and just when Thornhill, junior, successfully invades the family circle (he is to be Alexander the Great at the bottom of the painting), this scene highlights the falsely emblematic activity that betrays and exemplifies the moral flaw of our Job. Just before Olivia is taken, the vicar judges the relative value of the ballad and ode, condemning those odes that "petrify us in a single stanza." The line applies all too well to Primrose's ironic situation as expressed in the grand family portrait.

The transition from scene to sentiment, from emblem to expression, begins with the news of Olivia's abduction. When Primrose learns that his daughter has been taken, a Job scene is played out with a significant reversal. His nature gets the better of him and he immediately curses his oppressor, only to be brought back to his paradigmatic role by his wife and son. (This bears comparison to Parson Adams's reaction to news of his boy's "drowning" in *Joseph Andrews*.) The passionate outburst by our hero, however, marks a definite progress in Primrose's move toward the sublime, although the description of the family's grief reminds us that the Primroses are still described in *scenic* terms (to use another of Kenneth Burke's useful concepts). Thus we are told:

> In this manner that night the first of our real misfortunes was spent in the bitterness of complaint. . . . The next morning we missed our wretched child at breakfast where she used to give life and cheerfulness to us all.

Olivia is perceived as part of a breakfast picture; the scenic and the passionate coexist here. Only gradually will the latter come to dominate.

In the following chapter our narrator-hero recognizes that he may have been deceived as to the identity of the true villain. This is a crucial advance for Primrose, as he begins to recognize the fallibility of his constructions. In his meeting with the company of actors he is shown to appreciate the matter of false imitation as he discourses on the theater. False imitation, too, is the theme of the political harangue that Primrose delivers (tyranny masquerades as liberty, according to the agitated vicar), as well as of the disguise of Arnold's butler. Passion dominates the scene when George, the vicar's son, emerges from the company. The pattern of discovery, of emergence from a scene, is repeated in the discovery of Olivia at the inn. Whatever the literary success of Goldsmith's chain of events, we should bear in mind the contrast of the active, ironic creator of scenes, which our narrator is in the book's first half, and the suffering, passionate figure of the book's second half. The inns and rooms, the *frames* of the latter half, are utterly beyond the vicar's control.

The burning of Primrose's house underscores this development. It can be seen as the continuation of the Job motif (in the Bible, Satan is given dominion first over Job's property, then over his family, and finally over Job himself), but it is clearly much more than that. The biblical Job bears no real human relationship to his surroundings, but it is just this relationship that is the subject of Goldsmith's fiction. Crucially, the destruction of the Primrose house is not the beginning of punishment (as it was for Job) so much as the confirmation of a process of salvation that involves a new awareness of the meaning of human and social frames. The burn on the arm, another Job-parallel, is similarly reversed. The sentimental outburst by the vicar following the fire provides an interesting reversal of the biblical *complaint* and a demonstration of a new, passionate perception:

> Observe this bed of straw and unsheltering roof; those mouldering walls and humid floor; my wretched body thus disabled by fire, and my children weeping round me for bread: you have come home, my child, to all this; yet here, even here, you see a man that would not for a thousand worlds exchange situations. Oh, my children, if you could but learn to commune with your hearts, and know what noble company you can make them, you would little regard the elegance and splendour of the worthless.

The culminating revaluation of frames comes in the jail scene. Goldsmith emphasizes the frame aspect of the prison: we see two cells, the general cell, "strongly grated and paved with stone," and the individual cell. It is here, outside of society and away from the false self-dramatization of social framing, that the vicar is most sublime and most passionate. He establishes his society on faith and natural law, not on ceremony. He rejects the idea that property is founded in natural law, and argues that laws should reward as well as punish. The family visiting the vicar, says Primrose, "can make a dungeon seem a palace." Their intrinsic *humanity* now defines them, rather than their self-conscious existence in society.

Finally, after resigning himself to his death and the death of his son, Primrose becomes the center of a culminating transformation of the social frame. At the end of chapter 28 a pathetic scene is presented; Primrose rises to deliver his sermon:

> Thus saying, I made an effort to rise from my straw, but wanted strength, and was able only to recline against the wall. The prisoners assembled themselves according to my directions, for they loved to hear my counsel: my son and his mother supported me on either side; I looked and saw that none were wanting, and then addressed them with the following exhortation.

This is certainly a frame, but it takes us not to the false emblems of the first half of the *The Vicar*, but to its biblical analogue in Exodus 17:12, where Moses' hands are held up by Aaron and Hur. As Meyer Schapiro has shown, this scene has a rich iconographic history: Moses' outstretched arms were taken to figure the sign of the Cross (*Words and Pictures: On the Literal and the Symbolic in the Illustration of a Text*). Thus the artificial self-framing of which our hero was guilty has now reached an opposite extreme. Helped by others, he transcends his scene and delivers his moving sermon. Scene and passion now define one another, and the frame is wholly natural, based entirely on the love of his family and his fellow prisoners. The message of his sermon is therefore doubly appropriate for our transformed (and transfigured) hero:

> No vain efforts of a refined imagination can soothe the wants of nature, can give elastic sweetness to the dank vapours of a dungeon or ease to the throbbings of a broken heart.

Primrose's closing sermon preaches a doctrine of love. Indeed, *The Vicar of Wakefield* is Goldsmith's artistic elaboration of the sublime of love. That Goldsmith considered love and the sublime inseparable can be seen in his review of [Edmund] Burke's *A Philosophical Inquiry into the Origin of Our Ideas of the Sublime and Beautiful* in the *Monthly Review* for May

1757. In an otherwise favorable notice, Goldsmith suggested that the author had not sufficiently considered love as an element of the sublime:

> Our Author by assigning terror for the only source of the sublime excludes love, admiration &c. But to make the sublime an idea incompatible with those affections is what the general sense of mankind will be apt to contradict. . . . Our astonishment at the sublime as often proceeds from an increased love as from an increased fear.

It is precisely the sublime of love that is attained by the end of the novel.

IV

There is a change, then, that corresponds to the break in the book after chapter 17. That the change relates to Job is undeniable, but that it follows Battestin's theological reconstruction is less likely. Even after the sublime climax in chapter 29, Goldsmith plays with the biblical paradigm:

> The greatest object in the universe, says a certain philosopher, is a good man struggling with adversity, yet there is still a greater which is the good man that comes to relieve it.

This sentiment is as close to romance motifs as it is distant from the point of the Book of Job. And the title of chapter 30, we recall ("Let us be inflexible and fortune will at last change in our favour"), seems to have forgotten the lesson of the earlier chapter.

Goldsmith's use of a biblical type is thus complex in *The Vicar*. Overall, we can say that his free use of the Book of Job, and his emphasis upon a contrast between scene and sentiment, parallels in important ways new biblical-critical notions of the sublimity of the Hebrew poetry and the particular, detheologized sublimity of Job in the works of Lowth and contemporary Semiticists. England's reception of biblical criticism was very halting: Lowth's primary influence on later work in England comes indirectly by way of Michaelis, Herder, and the German romantics. But that the Bible was sublime and was a species of Oriental literature was widely accepted. We don't know Goldsmith's precise acquaintance with the work of Lowth, but an Orientalizer like Goldsmith would certainly have been receptive to his very popular ideas. Our author's use of Job, then, is to give us a *human* rather than a *divine* message, and that message has much less to do with how we will fare in the next world than it has to do with how we ought to act and to know ourselves in this one.

CHARLES A. KNIGHT

Ironic Loneliness: The Case of Goldsmith's Chinaman

One imagines that the *eiron*, like the prophet, undergoes an initiation of fasting, mortification, and prayer. One pictures him arriving from the desert, bringing a vision of the truth of human nature that is all the more perturbing for being secular rather than divine. If that vision is born of an experience somehow more intense and troubled than the illusions of common folk, it seems all the more strongly to isolate him from the rest of us. The literary and philosophical history of ironists—real, mythical, and fictional—is the record of that ironic loneliness. Democritus, the laughing philosopher, as Robert Burton translates his story, lived by himself and was thought mad by the townspeople (*Anatomy of Melancholy*). Though Lucian probably did not, as the early Christians supposed, meet his just fate from mad dogs, as the narrator of "The Death of Peregrinus" he almost earned his public death from the followers of his deluded victim, and he decided to vent the full force of his ironies in a quasi-private letter to a friend. Socrates, who in a real sense was executed because he was an ironist, ironically tried to turn the tables and suggest that the reason for his condemnation was the satiric attack of Aristophanes. Even in the urbane eighteenth century the fate of Swift, exiled to his Deanery supposedly because the Queen disliked (and misread) *A Tale of a Tub*, illustrated the potential fate of ironists—misunderstanding and rejection.

But if we see the ironist as isolated and cast out by the hatred of his victims, by our distrust of his methods of entrapment, and by our fear that

From *Journal of English and Germanic Philology* 82, no. 3 (July 1983). © 1983 by the Board of Trustees of the University of Illinois.

he may know more about us than we know ourselves, that prophetic image
of the ironist must be balanced by its alternate, wherein it is not he but the
alazon, the pretentious fool, who is the isolated individual. The eiron, therefore, speaks with the voice of social responsibility. We identify with his
cause and delight in its result; we take pleasure in the discomfiture of the
ironic victim, and we are relieved that we are not the victim. If the prophetic
eiron champions the uncompromising norms of the individual against social
corruption, which he identifies as pandemic vice or folly, the social ironist
(the eiron as priest, not prophet) articulates the values of a healthy and
aware community when he identifies the eccentricities of the inflated individual. Moliere provides notable instances of both in *Le Misanthrope*.
Philinte's view of society, though more cynical and negative than Alceste's,
allows him to preserve the valuable aspects of human relations by enduring
the perversions of folly. He thus approximates the social ironist. Alceste, of
course, rejects that society, even with its infrequent goods, in favor of the
eiron's prophetic absolutism.

These two contrasting images, apparently irreconcilable, can be balanced or even united in a number of ways. Moliere, as the dramatic author
capable of presenting both Philinte and Alceste in their unresolved conflict,
serves as one model for such balance—that, perhaps, of a dramatic neutral-
ity. Socratic irony also neutralizes the conflict. By adopting the position of
genuine self-criticism, one cannot claim the absolutism of an Alceste, though
one's attack on society is no less devastating and total. In making that
attack, however, one claims to defend the interests of the community, despite the anger of its citizens: it is Socrates rather than Meletus who is the
true lover of Athens. But however these two separate images of the ironist
may be joined, like the images in a range finder when the focus is achieved,
the personal problem is not resolved, as the fate of Socrates himself suggests.
The relationship between social community and social isolation is a delicate
manifestation of the tension between the ironist as the perceiver of discom-
forting and even threatening human truths and the human needs of the
ironist himself.

The conclusion of Goldsmith's *Citizen of the World* is a particularly
complex example of the loneliness of the eiron, just as the periodical itself
is a particularly rich exploration of the ironist's relation to the society he
observes. The final letter of Lien Chi's series describes the resolution of the
periodical's framing story. His son, Hingpo, has rescued a distressed maiden
from a sultan's harem, and both have fled. They have become separated, but
as it turns out, Zelis, the maiden, just happens to be the niece of Lien Chi's
best friend, the Man in Black. The two young people will now get married,

and in so doing they potentially provide Lien Chi, the Chinaman whose letters constitute the series, with a home and country which he lost at the opening. In the manner of comic resolutions, the Man in Black—the work's sentimental misanthrope—will also wed.

But though the romantic frame plot reaches a conventional closure in marriage, the periodical series itself can reach no such romantic climax. Unlike the novel, but like the real life from which it flows, the periodical comes to no conclusion but merely ends when the author takes his leave. *The Citizen of the World* casts off the possibilities of a comic and novelistic ending for the irresolution of a periodic one. Lien Chi, the traveler, ironist, and philosopher, will continue his travels, though to do so means that he must reject the family unity that the romantic ending has suddenly made possible. The Man in Black reinforces this ambiguous conclusion: his projected marriage fails to take place because of last-minute incompatibility, and he joins Lien Chi, in many respects his alter ego, in his travels.

But if the conclusion emphasizes the loneliness of the cosmopolitan man (seeing all things, he belongs to none), the work as a whole proclaims the dignity and charm of his *metier*. For through the range and diversity of his periodical letters he strives to achieve that necessarily shifting perspective from which all things can be truly seen. And if in exploring the parochialism of the British he sometimes reveals his Chinese narrowness, he seeks to find the universality of human experience by reflecting upon his travels. If at times he fails or seems foolish himself, his continual power to capture astonishing and revealing images of ourselves engages us in a rewarding exploration of human unity and diversity. And our efforts to follow his lead instruct us in a similar adroitness of vision.

This adroitness is not always welcome. William Hazlitt notes the effect, though he is not happy with it. *The Citizen of the World*, he writes,

> contrives to give an abstracted and somewhat perplexing view of things, by opposing foreign prepossessions to our own, and thus stripping objects of their customary disguises. Whether truth is elicited in this collision of contrary absurdities, I do not know; but I confess the process is too ambiguous and full of intricacy to be very amusing to my plain understanding. For light summer reading, it is like walking in a garden full of traps and pitfalls.
> (*Lectures on the English Comic Writers*)

Twentieth-century readers may be more likely than Hazlitt to find such walking invigorating and to seek possible truths in "contrary absurdities." But Hazlitt's cautionary admission of the perplexing qualities of Goldsmith's essay series is an important place to begin defining the essential qualities of that complex work and of its ironic observer, for the radical charge that Hazlitt makes against Lien Chi is that perplexity is at the center of *The Citizen of the World*, or rather that there is no such center, but merely a series of surface ironies that circle upon each other like a cat chasing its tail. The problem of the foreign observer, Hazlitt seems to claim, is that his lonely perspective merely collides with ours and that the positions do not instructively engage. By remaining unreconciled, the observer continues in his ironic loneliness.

The root of the problem may well be an uncertainty as to whether Lien Chi speaks with the voice of his author or, as Robert H. Hopkins has argued, is himself a consistent ironic victim. Or if he is neither one nor the other in a consistent pattern, it may be the reader, unable to arrive at a clear interpretation, who becomes the ironic victim. But when we turn, as seems appropriate, from Lien Chi to Goldsmith, we become caught in the historic ambiguity with which Goldsmith himself has been regarded from the eighteenth century to the present.

There are certainly substantial grounds for identifying Lien Chi, at least to some degree, with his creator. He embodies a recurrent theme of Goldsmith's major works—that of the traveller who observes and sympathizes with the world, only to discover, like the speakers of *The Traveller* and *The Deserted Village*, that the familial home is gone and domestic happiness no longer seems attainable in the wanderer's life, though he observes its possibility in the lives of others. By 1759, when the "Chinese Letters" began to appear in Newbery's *Public Ledger*, Goldsmith had left Ireland, having failed to take orders, had studied medicine in Edinburgh, had pursued further study in Leyden and Paris, had traveled the continent rather like George Primrose in *The Vicar of Wakefield*, had set up as a physician and failed, had failed in his famous stint as a tutor in Peckham, and had managed to find a minimal livelihood as a hack writer. Like Lien Chi he could no longer return home, and he was a foreigner in England—more an observer than a participant in events. His travels had given him a cosmopolitan acquaintance with the world of learning, which he had displayed with some success in his *Enquiry into the Present State of Polite Learning in Europe* (1759). Lien Chi's roles as the philosophical traveler, the ironic commenter on a society which he sees from the fringe, and the sentimental recorder of a human condition whose woes he also suffers are all roles that Goldsmith shared.

But he shared as well the ambiguities of Lien Chi's portrait. Lien Chi is first presented to us in terms that make him an ideal and reliable persona for

Goldsmith's series. Letter 1, written by an Amsterdam merchant, recommends him as an honest man, a philosopher by reputation, knowledgeable in the English language but ignorant of English customs. But Lien Chi nonetheless appears foolish on occasion. Part of that foolishness is the awkwardness of the outsider or the naivete of a man who is imposed upon by cheats he lacks the knowledge to detect. But as Hopkins has noted, Lien Chi tends to be less reliable the more he is Chinese. His character as a Chinaman is itself an elaborate hoax. He insists on it vigorously when he is satirizing the *chinoiserie* of the English; he drops it entirely for many of his more serious papers; and he shows at times a familiarity with English life which a far more seasoned visitor could hardly achieve. But when he corresponds on specific Chinese matters, he tends toward platitude and inconsistency. Like many fathers, he is especially sententious in addressing advice to his son, and on those occasions he often echoes conventional wisdom. Thus, like Goldsmith himself, he is the wise and good man who often falls into folly, and the question in interpreting his character, like that of his creator, is the degree to which that folly is recognized and controlled, to which it is the conscious posing of the eiron rather than the lapses of an alazon.

Quintana suggests that *The Citizen of the World* is "a one way street," for while we form an idea of Lien Chi's character, we never seem him through the eyes of those whom he sees (as contrasted to Goldsmith himself, of whom we have many conflicting images). In the main this is true, though we certainly see him (but darkly) through the eyes of his editor, of the Amsterdam merchant who introduces us, and through such occasional characters as the English lady of letter 14 ("What an unusual share of *somethingness* in his whole appearance"), whose false notions of Chinese matters cannot be dislodged by the testimony of a "real" Chinaman. But the rhetorical structure of *The Citizen of the World* extends beyond the use of a persona and that extension complicates the involvement of Goldsmith in the paper.

The traditional periodical essay, modeled on the *Spectator*, included in its fictional rhetoric a club or similar set of assistants to the editor-author, and one of the major functions of that club was to serve as an extension of the fictitious author himself. But the members of that club in turn became the objects of the author's observation. Thus the periodical could suggest a double vision: its *eidolon* or personified author functioned as the agent of observation; fragmented into the further personified members of the club, his qualities, or those of the paper he represents, could serve as observed objects. The club therefore became a reflective mirror. Such mirroring functions remain in two aspects of *The Citizen of the World*—in the frame story concerning Lien Chi's son Hingpo (a family was a frequent alternative to the club, projecting the eidolon's personality through family resemblances rather than through the affinities of friendship), and in the small cast of characters who reappear in a number of papers. Primary among these characters are the Man in Black (who first appears in letter 13) and Beau Tibbs (letter 54). Both are extensions not only of Lien Chi's character but that of his creator.

Like Lien Chi, the Man in Black embodies a conflict between, on one hand, a hardened stoicism in the face of the vicissitudes of life and the evils of human nature and, on the other, a warm and sentimental compassion for the miseries of others. In the case of Lien Chi this conflict is represented by his oriental stoicism, by his compassionate nature, and by the conclusions on the value of human sympathy that he has drawn from his observations (letter 23). For the Man in Black the conflict emerges from his own personal history, as described in letters 26 and 27. Though he is generous and loving by nature and early training, he professes himself to be parsimonious and misanthropic, a position he has been forced to assume by a combination of misfortune and his own imprudence in money matters. The details of the life of the Man in Black correspond with those of Goldsmith's own history, and their inclusion in the character's story has served as a signal of Goldsmith's identification with him. Insofar as he represents Goldsmith, then, he provides a means of self-perception and self-apology, a way in which Goldsmith can reveal himself within the defenses of a fictional construct.

The Man in Black is a complex character, and he is presented to us through a complex perspective. The ironic inconsistencies of his character are transmuted into a verbal irony. At the end of letter 27 he sets forth (in Lien Chi's appropriate italics) the paradoxical conclusion to which his experience has brought him: "The truest way of finding esteem even from the indigent, is *to give away nothing, and thus have much in our power to give.*" But if we see him as the rather transparent victim of his own illusions, we also see him as a good man, with whose personality we sympathize. We understand his motives, even while we smile at his behavior, and we come to share the sense of the harshness of experience that forces him to put on his ridiculous mask. Because we view him with both sympathy and irony, he becomes a lovable eccentric whose motives and behavior we judge separately.

The Man in Black was born at virtually the same literary moment as Toby Shandy. (Volumes 1 and 2 of *Tristram Shandy* were published in January 1760; the Man in Black first appeared in the *Public Ledger* of 25 February 1760.) Though Lien Chi is offended by the pert bawdry of Sterne's novel (letter 53), the basic profile of the humorist appears in both works. Lien Chi describes his friend as "an humourist in a nation of humourists" (letter 26), and the Man in Black's character is compounded, in roughly equal parts, of the amiable and the ridiculous. Though Uncle Toby lacks the misanthropic contrast to a kind heart, its equivalent is to be found in his military hobbyhorse. The key to these characters lies not only in their own peculiar mixture of the head and the heart but in the way in which the reader is required to exercise those organs. Irony has perhaps never been a merely intellectual exercise: certainly the reader's emotional disgust at the cannibalism of *A Modest Proposal* is an important guide to an intellectual analysis. But in the cases of both Uncle Toby and the Man in Black (and, I would argue, of Dr. Primrose) the judgments of the head and the sentiments of the heart pull in different directions. The ambiguities of the ironist, the tension between isolation and community, between rejection and acceptance, reemerge in the perplexities of the humorist, whose presence in the person of the Man in Black allows Lien Chi, the ironist, to observe and contemplate the ironies of his own position.

The case of Beau Tibbs is, if anything, more perplexing. He is less clearly a sympathetic character than the Man in Black, and his identification with Goldsmith is less certain. Indeed, if the Man in Black shares some of the more attractive elements of Goldsmith's follies, Beau Tibbs shares some of the least. (It may be no accident that when Sir Joshua Reynolds came to paint Goldsmith's portrait in 1766, he chose to clothe him in the dignified apparel of the Man in Black rather than the dandified outfit of Beau Tibbs.) Goldsmith shared with the Beau his foolish ostentation of dress. One contemporary reportedly described him—in full regalia, including sword—as "that fly with a pin stuck through it," and stories of his profligate spending on clothes recur in the early biographies. The contrast between Beau Tibbs's dress and his circumstances parallels Goldsmith's, and it is tempting to speculate that the sorry garret where the Beau and his wife reside is based on Goldsmith's own lodgings in Green Arbour Court, from which he moved during the initial run of the "Chinese Letters." Like both Goldsmith and the Man in Black, Beau Tibbs is imprudent in money matters, and at their first meeting, after considerable name-dropping and pretense that he is a person of significance, he asks for money. Most telling of all is the exhibition of petty self-importance that resounds through contemporary accounts of Goldsmith, as it does through Lien Chi's account of Beau Tibbs.

When the dandified beau and the outlandish Chinaman walk together through St. James's Park, they are the source of understandable amusement to the passers-by. Beau Tibbs's defenses against such ridicule are impenetrable. When Lien Chi faces him with it directly, he passes it off as an ironist's impulse to play the fool: *"but, blast me, when the world laughs at me, I laugh at the world, and so we are even. My Lord Trip, Bill Squash, the Creolian, and I sometimes make a party at being ridiculous"* (letter 55). If this partial identification of Beau Tibbs with Goldsmith is accurate, Goldsmith seems to embark on a remarkable and daring venture of ironic self-exploration, for both the self as ironic observer and the self as ironic victim are present in the text, and the victim's self-accepting defense is that of the ironist as well.

The divergent interpretations of Goldsmith's personality perhaps present a false dichotomy. His detractors, such as Boswell (at times), saw him as a fool whose ability to write such brilliant and endearing works was something of a *lusus naturae*. His defenders argue that his character has been misread, that beneath the garrulous front of Irish folly was a subtle ironist willing to use himself as the illustrative ironic victim. The two alternatives are not really exclusive. If one is at times capable of a self-directed humor, one may on other occasions be unaware of one's own folly. The mask of comedy may at times become indistinguishable from one's own face. The important point is that in *The Citizen of the World* Goldsmith was able to use the fictional rhetoric of the periodical essay in such a way as to create an elaborate self-projection, within which he could be both the ironic observer and the character observed. Thus he forms the inconsistencies of his own character into a controlled fictional artifact.

One element of that control, however, is the play of ironic perception, and if that irony is to be fruitful, it must lead to some greater clarity than the unresolved contention of "contrary absurdities." Hence we must ask whether, to borrow Hazlitt's terms, Goldsmith provides us with appropriate warnings to locate his potentially destructive "traps and pitfalls." But in considering that question, we must be aware of a substantial distinction between *The Citizen of the World* and many other ironic works. *The Citizen of the World* shares identifying characteristics with two distinctly different satiric genres, the foreign-observer satire and the periodical essay. These genres perpetuate the alternative images of the eiron as prophet, attacking from outside the practicing values of the community, and the eiron as priest, articulating its values. The generic assumptions of the periodical essay would seem to point toward a straightforward reading of the Chinaman as a reliable but eccentric observer commenting on the peculiarities of English life, within a series of separate papers whose vague governing purpose comprises a practical moral commentary mixed with a gentle, good-humored satire of manners. But the fictional aspects of *The Citizen of the World*, in particular its frame story and the characterization of its speaker, point to the ironic satire provided by an outsider, an observer concerned to explore the contradictions of social nature rather than an insider who laughs with us at our follies. Goldsmith's dual treatment of his ironist is echoed by the ambiguities of his generic assumptions.

But though Lien Chi shares many of the important features of the foreign observer, he differs from some of the most notable models in that tradition. In *Lettres Persanes*, certainly a conscious model for Goldsmith, Montesquieu's observant Persians, Usbek, Rica, and Rhedi, like Lien Chi, discourse upon a variety of topics, and their character as observers is generally complex. Though they speak, especially Usbek, as thoughtful men of reason, they are caught, as are the French they observe, by the imperfections of their own society, and at the end the melodramatic collapse of Usbek's harem manifests the failure of his autocratic practices to take account of the human nature of his concubines in his absence. Montesquieu spends considerably more time in his frame story and on exploiting the exotic possibilities of his letter writers than does Goldsmith. Indeed, the equivalent of the dénouement of *Lettres Persanes* takes place in letter 6 of *The Citizen of the World*, in which Lien Chi learns that the result of his absence has been the imprisonment of his family (with the exception of his son, who goes forth in quest of his father) and the loss of his estate. His philosophical resignation in the face of this disaster may be, as Hopkins suggests, an indication of the absurdity of his belief that knowledge will lead to happiness, but it also reinforces his isolation as a traveler and observer. Goldsmith's treatment of Lien Chi rejects the pattern of development in *Lettres Persanes* in which the increasingly pessimistic observations of the Persians are mirrored by the collapse of the world they have left behind. Though Lien Chi can never return to his home, as the series progresses he becomes reconciled to his condition as a traveler and ends by embracing it willingly.

A particularly strong divergence of *The Citizen of the World* from the foreign-observer genre is its movement toward the periodical essay. In its initial run it was envisioned and essentially read as a series of individual papers, each a satisfying and complete unit. That sequence was extended over a period of twenty months, so that the search for large architectural structures does not seem an appropriate approach to the work. The individual essays, like those of many similar series, focus on a single incident, on a single point or line of argument, or on a single compressed narrative. This singleness of subject not only reflects the limitations of length that preclude extensive, detailed, and complex explorations of complex subjects but reflects as well the periodicity that marks out each essay as discrete in time—separate and individual.

Goldsmith uses several means to transcend somewhat the individuation of separate essays. He often links essays in pairs on the basis of similiar subject matter, especially in the bound version of the series. Though his frame story is slow to unfold and is substantially less dominant than Montesquieu's in *Lettres Persanes*, framing is an unusual feature for a periodical essay, pointing to a fictional conclusion rather than a periodical leavetaking. The persisting presence of Lien Chi as speaker is another such connecting device, as is the fact that most of his letters are written to the same correspondent (unlike the different correspondents of *Lettres Persanes*). A further degree of consistency in subject and tone is achieved through the beginning nearly one-third of the papers with a distinct comparison of Chinese or Oriental life or institutions to those of the English, thus reinforcing the foreign-observer motif.

But despite these gestures toward a partial coherence, the periodical characteristics of the series account for the variety of roles in which Lien Chi is cast. In some cases he is a naïve observer; in others his foreign perspective gives him a keen perception of irony, which he shares with the reader. His philosophical comments are at times cribbed from such Oriental sources as Goldsmith had at hand. His diversity of roles makes it difficult to characterize him in more than general terms. But it also suggests that the key to Goldsmith's irony lies in the reader's perception of local signals of ironic intent rather than in the reading of a cumulative and consistent character in the speaker.

The question of ironic intent in *The Citizen of the World* is not whether the speaker is ironic or not, but when and under what circumstances he is ironic. How are we to know whether Lien Chi is ironic and whether these ironies are under his conscious control? Looking at the work from the extreme of periodicity, one could perhaps argue that each essay contains the circumstances and conditions of its own irony, in which case the reader is left only with the warning to be alert. But though considerable variety in ironic stance is possible, Goldsmith employs a series of particular patterns that are clear enough to serve as more-or-less reliable signals of ironic intent.

These ironic signals depend upon two basic patterns of irony. One of these is the traditional eiron-alazon relationship, the relation, for example, between Lien Chi and Beau Tibbs, between the perceptive observer and the pretentious fool. The role of eiron is generally established in the series through its use of a foreign observer. The mere presence of Lien Chi as the observer of English customs tends to suggest an ironic mode of presentation. Hence he can function as a silent eiron when, as in letter 4 (on English pride and liberty) or in letters 29 and 30 (describing a club of authors), he needs only to set down the foolishness of others, with minimal comment. But this capacity to bestow irony through perceiving and recording folly is limited to Lien Chi's specific observation of behavior and to those papers that fall clearly in the foreign-observer genre. He is not usually ironic when the material he discusses is moral and philosophical in nature. In fact the expectation (established at the outset by the letter introducing him) that Lien Chi's values will be more or less solid is necessary to the reader's willingness to appreciate him as a perceptive ironist.

The ironic signals become complicated when the roles of eiron and alazon are joined to a second ironic pattern, the manipulation of internal and external speakers. In the usual pattern Lien Chi serves as the external or ironic speaker and, as in the case of letter 4, for example, the inner speakers are the foolish voices whose folly is made all the more apparent by being recorded. But this pattern is capable of canny and effective variations.

One such variation occurs when the factor of periodicity, with its temporal separation of discrete units, allows Lien Chi to serve as both eiron and alazon. The result is a pattern of illusion and disillusion in which the knowledge brought by disillusion allows Lien Chi to reflect upon his own behavior. Letter 8 begins as if continuing the theme of a previous letter (letter 3) on the differences between English and Chinese concepts of feminine beauty. Lien Chi admits that despite these differences he is taken by the attractive manner of English women—"so free, so pressing, so hospitable, and so engaging." It is soon clear that he is actually talking about prostitutes, but he elevates their invitations to a high moral plane. The general description of their attentions settles down to the visit of "one of those generous creatures" to Lien Chi's apartment, where she sees a watch and takes it with her, ostensibly to be fixed. Lien Chi is most elaborate in his oriental expressions of gratitude. But at the beginning of letter 9 he announces a recognition of his deception: "I have lost a trifle, I have gain'd the consolation of having discovered a deceiver," and therefore, "the present moment becomes a comment on the past, and I improve rather in humility than wisdom."

Humility and the lack of pretense to wisdom are, of course, the classic qualities of the eiron. For the reader the pattern is more complex. We are aware from the beginning that Lien Chi's inferences about the ladies are wrong, and the admission of his mistake in the next paper confirms this awareness, allowing us to savor the superiority of our perception, though we are also aware that we too are at times the innocent victims of our misconceptions. But the second paper also reinforces our good opinion of the Chinaman: he may be wrong, but he is not foolish. The movement in time from illusion to discovery is thus a corrective process that validates rather than undercuts his general trustworthiness.

That trust is more severely tested when the roles of eiron and alazon are applied to Lien Chi simultaneously rather than being separated in time or split into separate characters. In letter 119, Lien Chi records "the distresses of a common soldier," and the pattern of internal and external speakers suggests a regular eiron-alazon relationship. Certainly the soldier seems an ironic victim, for he responds to his story of unremitting woe and exploitation with an apparently naïve patriotism and a detached *sang-froid*. He tells his tale "with an intrepidity truly British"; he owns that Newgate prison was "as agreeable a place as ever I was in all my life"; and he asserts that despite his loss of four fingers and one leg he is in good health and "will for ever love liberty and Old England." But the essay is presented not as an example of the shocking conditions whereby brave soldiers are reduced to beggary but as an instance of a purely brave man who can endure private misery. At the end the soldier limps off, "leaving my friend and me in admiration at his intrepidity and content; nor could we avoid acknowledging, that an habitual acquaintance with misery is the truest school of fortitude and philosophy." (Letter 119 did not appear in the *Public Ledger* but was added to the work in its volume publication; hence in its original version [in the *British Magazine* of June 1760] it did not have Lien Chi as a dramatized outer speaker but only the anonymous essayist.)

Thus at the end of the essay Lien Chi seems to return to the conventional wisdom with which he had begun, without any awareness of how that wisdom has been compromised by what he has recorded. The question is whether his silence is the cunning of the ironist or the blindness of an ironic victim. The ironic intention of the author is evident, as is the identification of the reported or internal speaker as at least a partial ironic victim. The reader may therefore be in doubt as to whether Lien Chi, the fictitious essayist, is in control of his irony, and that doubt may threaten the sense of Lien Chi's reliability in other contexts as well. At this point two considerations are useful: (1) Lien Chi's silence is necessary to preserve the reader's role in deciphering the irony, for one can hardly imagine an effective version of the essay in which the essayist joins the reader in condemning the soldier; (2) Lien Chi's views elsewhere in the work suggest that he would agree with the deciphering and the values it implies, for he is not sympathetic to the French war (letter 17) which the soldier supports so enthusiastically, and he frequently articulates the value of human sympathy, in contradition to the callousness of the soldier.

The complexity of the ironic voice in this instance thus prompts a complexity in the reader's outlook that is analogous to the way in which we look at the Man in Black and Beau Tibbs. We sympathize with the soldier's misfortunes; we are tempted to adopt his own values and to find him meritorious. But as we fill in Lien Chi's silence, we are reminded that we can share that position only to a point, and that behind the callousness of the soldier (itself the combination of bravery with despair) lies the callousness of a government that has brought him to this point. Thus in letter 119 both the internal and external speakers are partial victims of irony—but the external a calculating victim, I would argue. This dislocating mixture of ironies leads to several different but simultaneous levels of perception in the reader.

Less complex, perhaps, but almost equally dislocating is the function of the nearly invisible "editor," who in the "Preface" takes responsibility for anglicizing the Chinese letters and making them accessible to English readers. The editor's role is, of course, part of the game of chinoiserie, for he explains a patent fiction (that the letters are genuine) which the reader can accept in good fun without him. But on occasion the arrangement of internal and external speakers shifts so that Lien Chi, usually the outer speaker, becomes an inner speaker, with the editor serving as ironic commentator. The shift occurs especially in essays where Lien Chi's reflections apply to misfortunes in the frame story, and the presence of irony is signalled by deprecating footnotes or prefatory comments by the editor, usually pointing out that the material is a "rhapsody" (i.e., a miscellany) of sentiments drawn from Confucius or some other Oriental source. Such shifting of speakers outward allows Lien Chi to be an occasional ironic victim without making the reader uncertain (as Hopkins seems to claim) of his general reliability. The editor's comments, though they establish Lien Chi as an ironic victim, also identify the occasions on which our suspicions should be aroused, and they tend to transfer the responsibility for ironic foolishness partially from Lien Chi to his Chinese sources, thus limiting the nature and instances of his folly. He becomes an ironic victim whose general trustworthiness is maintained, and his occasional appearance in this role reinforces his function as a foreign observer.

Because of this general trustworthiness, Lien Chi can confidently practice the usual ironic arts of overstatement and inappropriate evaluation. His Oriental tendency to hyperbole makes both arts appropriate to his character. In those frequent cases where irony results from an inappropriate rela-

tionship between words and their referents (as, for example, in his praise of
physicians in letter 68), Lien Chi seems in clear control of his language.
Though there may be particular instances in which particular readers may
be uncertain as to whether irony is intended, an uncertainty hardly avoid-
able in any work where the voice shifts so frequently from ironic to straightforward statements, the general pattern of Lien Chi's stances in relation to
his material seems readily perceptible.

That perceptibility is, of course, enhanced by the fact that in so many
straightforward papers he serves so clearly as the author's spokesman, as
the serious, philosophical commentator on issues of contemporary life: thus
he sincerely praises Voltaire (letter 43) and comments on the justice of Earl
Ferrar's execution (letter 38); he speculates seriously on historical patterns
in the decline of learning (letter 63) and warns against holding human
nature in too high esteem (letter 115). The reader's awareness of Lien Chi
as a controlling ironist is further reinforced by the various ironic functions
he assumes in the papers that begin the work, an opening series that seems
almost designed to instruct us in the mental gymnastics we will be called
upon to perform. The pattern of illusion and disillusion is exemplified in
letters 8 and 9, but before the reader has come to this pattern, he has seen
Lien Chi as a reliable ironic observer (letter 4) and as the editor's ironic
victim (letter 7). And letter 5—on English political passions and their product, the newspaper—reveals him as an adept practitioner of verbal irony.

The Citizen of the World thus achieves a clarity in its manipulation of
distinct ironic possibilities. Across the range of individual essays the
Chinaman assumes a number of positions that allow him to see from various angles. This variety of positions and the concomitant multiple signals of
irony are consistent with the individuation of essays, though the perception
of irony is at times dependent on the reader's general awareness of qualities
developed in other essays and in the series as a whole. But Lien Chi's
character is not novelistic. It reveals itself in the flashes of his own perception. To see him in developmental rather than segmental terms, or as specifically rather than generally consistent, is to apply without warrant to one
genre our expectations of another.

If one tries to see *The Citizen of the World* as a novel *manqué* whose
recurrent characters are struggling to achieve the full development possible
in fiction, the effects of periodicity will seem constraining: "The real trouble
was that Beau Tibbs and Vauxhall Gardens asked to be given a longer lease
on life, but the end of the column was reached; down came the shears, and
a new subject must be broached next week." But freed from the obligations
of plot and thematic coherence, the periodicalist and his spokesman enjoy

new possibilities for the observation of society and the exploration of human nature through the manipulation of ironic and serious perspectives. The possibilities are analogous to those Beethoven discovered in turning to the *Diabelli Variations* after the piano sonatas.

> Variation is potentially the most "open" of musical procedures, one which gives the greatest freedom to the composer's fantasy. It mirrors the unpredictability and chance nature of human expectation. . . . Variation is the form of shifting moods, alternatives of feeling, shades of meaning, dislocations of perspective. It shatters appearance into splinters of previously unperceived reality and, by an act of will, reassembles the fragments at the close.
>
> (Maynard Solomon, *Beethoven*)

The shifting perspective of the periodical essay provides a similar structural and epistemological principle. Because Lien Chi is less fully realized than the central character of a novel, he becomes especially open to a variety of emotions, thoughts, and experiences, just as the basic harmonic structure that takes the place of a theme in the *Goldberg Variations* allows Bach to compose a series of pieces encompassing an extraordinary range of musical expression. But in neither *The Citizen of the World* nor its musical analogues does the artist have to begin again at each periodic change in the form. Periodicity and variation share a mixture of recurrence and diversity. By virtue of Zeno's paradox of infinite divisibility, it is possible to choose from infinite possibilities within a finite range. The fictional elements of Lien Chi's character define that finite range, just as the periodicity of the series allows the infinite choice within it.

Lien Chi is characterized by definite and recurring traits: his social and intellectual curiosity, his Oriental propensity to overstatement, his foreigner's sense of newness and strangeness, his sympathy with the sufferings of the unfortunate, and his bemused impatience with pretentious nonsense. And he engages these qualities in a series of concerns that return, like the musical idea, throughout the variations afforded by his periodical medium. The shifting of perspectives made possible by periodicity involves not only changes in the ironic vantagepoint of the seer but also in the nature and position of the object seen. A series of characteristic topics runs through both the ironic and straightforward essays.

Lien Chi takes up and returns to a number of subjects of importance to the eighteenth century: the nature of sexual beauty and its relation to fashion, love, and moral goodness; the role of luxury in promoting the good or undermining the spirit of the state; the idea of the "great man," his nature and his merit, his occupation and his fame; the qualities of learning and the patterns of pretense to learning; war, trade, imperialism, and other political issues, especially in their relation to patterns of history. (One of the functions of Lien Chi's persona is that it gives Goldsmith's Tory views the aura of universal truth.) What Lien Chi tends to discover by considering such topics—through philosophical disquisition or narrative incident, through detailed observation or fable and allegory—is that when they are regarded by eyes whose focus has been broadened, as his own have been and as he hopes his readers' will be through his efforts, they reveal the relativity and subjectivity of things. Ideas of beauty depend upon culture; the great man is more the product of social fashion than of intrinsic merit; though luxury may in some historical periods bring the flourishing of culture, it also brings the danger of moral corruption. Hence reputation tends to replace reality, and the road to wisdom lies through the achievement of a practical and personal independence and through a tolerant and even skeptical philosophical objectivity. Indeed, these are the values Lien Chi affirms by continuing his travels at the end. The ironist's engagement in social issues reinforces his isolation.

Through the variety of its subjects and through its shifting ironic positions, the series repeatedly attempts to elicit from observation the basic qualities of human nature and society. The cosmopolite looks at provincial (i.e. English) manners and customs, measuring them on one hand by the sense of elemental human nature which his travels have taught him and on the other by his sense of the local, temporal, and ephemeral nature of social practices and ideas. His vision and the ironies it produces thus seek to separate the superficial from the substantial. In particular, he looks at human pretensions in relation to human character. At times, as in the case of the Man in Black, these pretensions are a device by which the pretender tries to control the excesses of his own personality or, as in the case of Beau Tibbs, seeks to avoid the destructive miseries of his condition. In both cases the result for the reader is a mixture of laughter and sympathy. For if these are not necessary illusions, they are useful ones, as perhaps Goldsmith knew well from his own experience. But though they may have their human value, such pretensions and illusions threaten, like the fear of mad dogs described in letter 69, to engulf reality.

The scope of material in *The Citizen of the World* and the play of its perspective create a complexly layered understanding of the human condition. At times the tension of divergent views produces a balance whose fulcrum is the "middle way" which Quintana found in Lien Chi's treatment of luxury. But at times the shifting weight of opinion seems to allow no resting point. By accepting what we are, we must accept as well the fluidity and flux of our situation. Surprisingly, for a work whose tone is so often that of comic geniality, there are virtually no happy people in it. Perhaps the nearest exemplar of the ordered, happy life is the philosophical cobbler of letter 65, Lucian's Micyllus fittingly transmigrated to eighteenth-century London, who disdains the chance to chase (as Lien Chi himself does) after idle shows and all they symbolize in order to profit from his own humble industry. But even he was burdened by an unhappy marriage. If no one's life is untroubled, the source of much human happiness, however incomplete, must lie in the achievement of an appropriate perspective, just as the source of much human folly lies in an inappropriate one.

Goldsmith's Chinaman is capable of embracing his ironic isolation both knowingly and willingly. His laughter is not that of scorn but a requisite for acceptance, including sympathy for the foolish as well as the recognition of folly. He neither abandons the world nor turns inwardly upon himself. As perpetual traveler he remains an ironist still—a prophet without divine revelation, a priest to a small band of initiated readers. He is the isolated man who seeks to return to community, and his social function is to create a world that is fit for human habitation. Such a world is not to be. By accepting its imperfect alternative but nonetheless asserting his detachment, by celebrating his son's marriage and then resuming his travels, he retains the unusual moral authority that lies in a mastery of the ways of seeing. By instructing us in the subtleties of his perspective, he offers us the possibilities of his independence and his reconciliation.

C. C. BARFOOT

The Deserted Village:
Goldsmith's Broken Circle

In a previous article, to which this is a companion, I suggested that it is only within the magic circle of the family or the extended family, the village, that Goldsmith or the narrator of *The Deserted Village* can allow himself to feel that art will not be used to deceive or to confuse, but be practised to attract souls to "brighter worlds," which will themselves be extensions of the innocence of childhood. I quoted a passage from *The Citizen of the World* in that article in order to indicate that Goldsmith is able to free words of possible guilty associations when they are used in the context of memories or evocations of "that spot in which we first had existence." I now wish to go a stage further and discuss the significance of Goldsmith's association of the form, image and emblem of the circle with the innocent allurement which as an essayist he attaches to "that spot which gave us birth" and as a poet he identifies with his "sweet Auburn." But first we have to begin not with *The Deserted Village* but with that earlier lyrical essay, *The Traveller,* which complements the later poem and in some ways antici- pates it by lamenting the state of exile that is a consequence of the act of dispossession that the inhabitants of Auburn suffer. In a manner of speaking *The Traveller* runs a circle of lamentation round *The Deserted Village,* which offers itself as a protective mandala that proves, alas, to be an empty mirage:

> But me, not destined such delights to share,
> My prime of life in wandering spent and care,

From *Dutch Quarterly Review of Anglo-American Letters* 13, no. 3 (1983). © 1983 by the *Dutch Quarterly Review of Anglo-American Letters.*

> Impelled, with steps unceasing, to pursue
> Some fleeting good, that mocks me with the view;
> That, *like the circle bounding earth and skies,*
> *Allures from far,* yet, as I follow, flies;
> My fortune leads to traverse realms alone,
> And find no spot of all the world my own.
>   (*The Traveller*, ll. 23–30, italics added)

In *The Deserted Village* the circle is not only present by way of theme, diction and imagery, but also stylistically and structurally. To take the last first, structural circularity is to be found in the handling of topics, which are laid down to be picked up again later, rather like a musical rondo movement; and is also to be observed in the balancing of one paragraph against another, as for instance in the first two which begin respectively:

> Sweet Auburn, loveliest village of the plain,
> Where health and plenty cheered the labouring swain,
>   (ll. 1–2)

and

> Sweet smiling village, loveliest of the lawn,
> Thy sports are fled and all thy charms withdrawn.
>   (ll. 35–36)

Here the repetition with variations of diction, phrasing and rhyme, and the contrast of tone and mood that results, suggest a return or restatement of a motif or a musical figure in a different key. The change of tense causes one to place the phrases that echo the past ("Sweet smiling village, loveliest of the lawn") in a context that denies that echo and indicates that the return is a matter of words only. Far from being a reassuring sign of continuity the repetition serves mainly to point a chilling contrast between past and present.

The repetition of the same or similar rhymes, which promises a renewal of experience like that recalled in the past, by virtue of the change of content serves to heighten one's realization that the past is no more, and that although the rhyme remains the same, circumstances have altered and the circle is broken:

> How often have I loitered o'er thy green,
> Where humble happiness endeared each scene.
>   (ll. 7–8)

Amidst thy bowers the tyrant's hand is seen,
And desolation saddens all thy green.
(ll. 37–38)

How often have I blessed the coming day,
When toil remitting lent its turn to play.
(ll. 15–16)

No more thy glassy brook reflects the day,
But, choked with sedges, works it weedy way.
(ll. 41–42)

The recurrence of the rhyme suggests a ghost or a circle, a might-have-been, hovering behind the tragic reality. Indeed the whole development of Goldsmith's lyrical style is towards a pattern of repetition which produces the impression of an obsessive recurrent strain in his thought and feelings. Sometimes the stylistic circularity is notably expressive, as in the line describing the reluctant farewells of the emigrants, who "returned and wept, and still returned to weep" (l. 369), before setting out in a westerly direction towards what may be imagined as a setting sun. (The "parting day" [l. 363] may be the day of departure or the day that is ending, or both.)

At the end of *Paradise Lost*, a poem which has evident associations with Goldsmith's, "the hastening angel" catches hold of "our lingering parents" in order to lead them "to the eastern gate." In *The Deserted Village* the poet places the same epithet, used by Milton to describe Adam and Eve's reluctant departure from Paradise, somewhat ambiguously in the second line of his second couplet:

Where smiling spring its earliest visit paid,
And parting summer's lingering blooms delayed.
(ll. 3–4)

Cunningly one is forced to linger on the word "lingering," not only by virtue of its phonetic echo ("ling"/"ring"), but also because of the uncertainty over its exact grammatical status; is it a noun ("parting summer's lingering") or is it an adjective ("lingering blooms delayed")? Even after many readings the grammar remains sufficiently ambiguous to cause more than a slight hesitation in the reader's attempt to place the caesura correctly in the line. This rhythmic indecision helps to emphasize the link between the beginning and the end of the poem, since it mimics both the reluctance of the season and of the blooms, and of the emigrants to depart. (The syntax of this couplet is also open to at least three possible readings. Probably to be discounted is that in which "spring" is to be taken as the subject of the verb "delayed" [as well as "paid"]; but we may well hesitate between a transitive interpretation of "delayed" [with "parting summer's lingering" as the subject] or an intransitive one [in which the whole phrase "parting summer's lingering blooms" is the subject of "delayed" = "tarried"]. One argument in favour of the latter is that it compels one to read "lingering" as an adjective, which thereby creates a triad of parallel phrases, "smiling spring," "parting summer" and "lingering blooms." One should also add that to the ear there is no difference between the "s" of a genitive ["summer's"] or of a plural [summers], which in effect ensures that for the listener at least a further ambiguity is brought into play.)

But *The Deserted Village* returns upon itself at the end only to signal the tragic change in a situation where the threatening billows of the sea and the prospect of "the rigours of the inclement clime" have replaced the Golden Age image of eternal spring which hovers behind Goldsmith's initial description of Auburn. Indeed Goldsmith's treatment of seasonal change at the beginning of the poem reconciles two apparently conflicting representations of nature's round: the traditional closed circle of Paradise, such as that established by Milton in book 4 of *Paradise Lost* (ll. 264–68), as well as the normal seasonal cycle, the type of all recurrent and circling change, which, in more than one sense, contains mutability by turning round upon itself in a process of repetition that is forever static and ever new.

The circle-motif is maintained throughout the first paragraph of *The Deserted Village* by larger and smaller details. The narrator himself does his round "pausing on every charm," including the "never failing brook" and "the busy mill," in themselves emblems respectively of perpetual natural and human activity. The concurrence of "talking age" and "whispering lovers" beneath the same hawthorn shade suggests the normal life-cycle of the village, while the regular pattern of work and play is introduced in terms of circular movement:

> How often have I blessed the coming day,
> When toil remitting lent its turn to play,
> And all the village train, from labour free,
> Led up their sports beneath the spreading tree;
> While many a pastime circled in the shade,
> The young contending as the old surveyed.
>
> (ll. 15–20)

There is some uncertainty about these lines as to whether they refer to an annual village holiday or an Irish Catholic Sunday, or something in frequency in between; however, the significant thing is that Goldsmith lays emphasis upon the repetition of the event and its regularity. Having referred to the unchanging patterns of activity in this opening paragraph and having linked the young to the old in lines 14 and 20, the poet deepens and extends the symbolic range of the lines by prompting us to take "the spreading tree" as also to refer to the generations which have played their games in this spot. For in this context the tree is not simply to be regarded as an apt inspirer of immemorial thoughts, but also as an appropriately traditional reminder of the family tree that joins the members of the extended village family together in the past as well as in the present.

Goldsmith's use of the tree, however natural and unselfconscious it may be, reminds one of Mircea Eliade's discussion of the "sacred power present in a tree," "a sacred tree" which is always to be found in "primitive conceptions of the 'sacred place' " that contains "the idea of 'centre,' of absolute reality": "the tree, with its periodic regeneration, manifested the power of the sacred in the order of life." Eliade goes on to talk about the "microcosmic landscape" that "gradually became reduced in time to but one of its constituents, to the most important: the tree or sacred pillar," which "came to express the cosmos fully in itself, by embodying, in apparently static form, its 'forces,' its life and its quality of periodic regeneration" (*Patterns in Comparative Religion*).

Goldsmith goes further in line 19 by suggesting that apart from the various games being played in the shade, "past-times" as well as "pastimes" are present as a shadow. We gather the hint that the old, who are said to be surveying the young (l. 20), are not just the aged people still living in Auburn but include inhabitants of the village from previous ages. Therefore in the first paragraph of the poem we are introduced to the notion of several different boundaries, enclosing different orders or groups, which, nevertheless, add up to a coherent whole. First we are reminded of the seasonal boundaries of the year; then we are conducted round the physical boundaries of the village; next we are introduced to the villagers as a group in which the generations are mingled within a single boundary; and finally it is suggested that the boundary of the village should be extended beyond the living to include the still observing dead. Auburn, potentially, consists not just of the present but also of time past and eternal time.

The mention of dancing and the game of the "smutted face" later in the first paragraph of *The Deserted Village* further develops the continuous metaphor and underlying emblem of the circle. The game, which is usually played in a ring and leads to "secret laughter" being "tittered round the place," acts as an innocent forewarning or an unconscious symbolic parody of the pollution that threatens the individual outside of the protective sphere of the village and an anticipation of the invading impurity that forces the villagers to emigrate.

But in the past "sleights of art and feats of strength went round":

> And still as each repeated pleasure tired,
> Succeeding sports the mirthful band inspired.
>
> (ll. 23–24)

Repetition and succession is emphasized once more a few lines later when the poet assures us that "sports like these, / With sweet succession taught e'en toil to please" (ll. 31–32), which again leads to an allusion, in a slightly odd way, to the continued potency of the past. "These round thy bowers their cheerful influence shed" (l. 33) can hardly be understood without some reference to the encompassing guardianship of the ancestors, here assimilated to the stars with which the phrase "shedding influence" is normally associated. The circular movement is then given stylistic reinforcement by the return of the first phrase from an earlier line (l. 31), which is twice repeated; the second time with the implication that this magic circle of the present and of various stages of the past, and of the living and the dead, is ended: "These were thy charms—But all thy charms are fled" (l. 34).

Literally and figuratively, the charm has been broken; which is another way of saying that the magic power identified with the social structure has been spilled and dissipated with the breaking up of that structure. One might have expected that Goldsmith would have made some later reference to the fate of the tree, which in the circumstances of the collapse of the village community, could be supposed to be felled or brought down by decay. In fact he does not do so, mainly no doubt because Goldsmith does not manipulate his symbols in an overt way, which would smack too closely of "the gloss of art," and like much else in *The Deserted Village* the tree means a great deal more than the poet consciously intended. However, its fall is covered by all the references to decline, collapse and destruction in the poem; and later the spreading tree and the hawthorn are exchanged for the less beneficent shadows of the gibbet in the city ("There the black gibbet glooms beside the way," l. 318) and the "matted woods" of America ("where birds forget to sing, / But silent bats in drowsy clusters cling," ll. 349–50).

The necessary centre and circumference of genuine communal relationships is described at many different places in the poem. In the village inn, with the serving maid also playing a traditional role, a ritualistic air asserts itself in the ceremonial drinking (ll. 247–50). Later Goldsmith ends his account of the girl reduced to freezing poverty in the city with the observation that "she left her wheel and robes of country brown" (l. 336). Here the primary reference is to her spinning wheel; but in view of the underlying motif of the circle in the poem, the familiar instrument of domestic industry takes on a deeper significance. For to work at the spinning wheel is not only to be part of a cycle of production taking place within the home, but also indicates a recognized stage in the traditional life cycle, hence the use of the word "spinster" for an unmarried woman. The spinning wheel may be understood as a representation of purity and virginity, with the home circle and the simple dress, unostentatious and generic, belonging to the class of all country girls in "robes of country brown." Goldsmith deliberately draws the attention of the reader to how the girl, having broken out of the normal run of things to be polluted and abandoned in the city, might have been blest in the village; and contrasts how, protected as primrose beneath the thorn, she might have adorned the cottage with her wretched situation "near her betrayer's door": once more emphasizing the security of the village compared with the double exclusion suffered by the outcast.

The circle appears in less solemn contexts. In the classroom, for instance, where "Full well the busy whisper, circling round / Conveyed the dismal tiding when he frowned" (ll. 203–4) and in the description of the gazing rustics round the schoolmaster, amazed "that one small head could carry all he knew" (l. 216). But in one of his most serious, not to say tragic, statements Goldsmith only alludes to a more explicit treatment of the motif.

One cannot be sure how far the first readers of *The Deserted Village* could be expected to fill out the allusion that Goldsmith makes in a pair of couplets to one of Dryden's finest and best known dedicatory epistles. But Goldsmith's lines expressing his vanished hopes of returning in his last days to the spot where he first had existence, for:

> As an hare, whom hounds and horns pursue,
> Pants to the place from whence at first she flew,
> I still had hopes, my long vexations past,
> Here to return—and die at home at last
>
> (ll. 93–96)

close the geometric figure less decisively than Dryden's:

> The Hare, in Pasture or in Plains is found,
> Emblem of Humane Life, who runs the Round;
> And, after all his wand'ring Ways are done,
> His Circle fills, and ends where he begun,

>   Just as the Setting meets the rising Sun.
>   ("To My Honour'd Kinsman, John Driden,"
>   ll. 62–66)

Goldsmith avoids the specific theological turn that Dryden's treatment of
the emblem implies; the later poet's version drops the allusion to the Resurrection, as if, despite his sympathetic portrait of the preacher, he no
longer looks for consolation or genuine redemption in religion. The extra-
terrestrial and extra-temporal spiritual power originally contained within
the greater boundary of the village has been lost with the loss of the earthly
village; and once the structure within which the spiritual power was benevo-
lently controlled has been broken up, religion is no longer to be looked for
as an aid. Yet perhaps Dryden's image of the setting meeting the rising sun
is responsible for the "metaphysical" impression given by Goldsmith's lines
at the end of the next paragraph, in which the retired wanderer bends:

>   To the grave with unperceived decay,
>   While resignation gently slopes the way;
>   And, all his prospects brightening to the last,
>   His Heaven commences ere the world be past!
>   (ll. 109–12)

This again suggests that life in the village and heavenly life may be conceived
of as being bound together within a single structure, and intimates a parallel
with the description of spring returning before summer had left with which
the poem begins. It is a true ring of eternity, a recurring pattern of close
relationships throughout life, which itself begins and ends in the same bliss-
ful spot, where the joining of generations is symbolized in the movements
and progression of sun and seasons and natural creatures.

But the image of the hare also reveals by implication the poet's dreadful
insecurity as he flees from hounds and horns to the village, where he looks
forward to drawing round him a protective circle of swains, who would
make him a focus of reassuring admiration. The hare's flight may be linked
with the false circle that may be found in *The Deserted Village* as a figu-
rative shadow, in which, in the words of *The Traveller*, the exile pursues
"some fleeting good," without success, and fails "to find / That bliss which
only centres in the mind" (l. 26 and ll. 423–24). This is a vexatious, pur-
poseless and phantasmagoric vicious circle. Rationalized, it can be detected
in the feverish pursuit of mercantile gain, when "Around the world each
needful product flies, / For all the luxuries the world supplies" (ll. 283–84),
which leads to the cosmopolitan movement of men and goods that destroys

the natural charmed boundaries of customary self-sufficient communities, and substitutes for them relationships based on the cash nexus. This circle, in which "rich men flock from all the world around" (l. 272), is evil because it represents an apparently formless, unstructured and unknowable world surrounding the inner ring of innocence, by which its threatening edges are defined.

More frequently, however, the contrary motion to purity and ease in *The Deserted Village* is conveyed by vertical rather than circular movement: by the opposition of "accumulation" and "decay," "flourishing" and "fading" (ll. 52–53), the second word in each of these pairs usually being the predominant one, and expressed as "fall" and "ruin." This type of contrast is common throughout:

> Sunk are thy bowers in shapeless ruin all,
> And the long grass o'ertops the mouldering wall;
> (ll. 47–48)

—where the downward progress of decay is manifest in the growth of grass and where the shapelessness of recent changes is set against the formal order of the past—or, for instance:

> Along the lawn, where scattered hamlets rose,
> Unwieldy wealth, and cumbrous pomp repose;
> (ll. 65–66)

—where a formless, amorphous and burdensome cessation of activity, after the feverish fret of acquiring riches, is to be contrasted with the genuine rest anticipated in line 88.

The contrast which Goldsmith makes in *The Deserted Village* between the circle and the line is supported by some remarks of John Barrell's on the effects of enclosure upon rural geography, in which he compares "the characteristically open-field sense of space—circular, restricted by the boundary of the parish" with "the landscape of parliamentary enclosure" which "expressed a more linear sense" (*The Idea of Landscape and the Sense of Place 1730-1840*). What Barrell has to say undoubtedly reflects the historical basis for Goldsmith's awareness of the weighty influence of topographical chance not only on social life but also on cosmological attitudes:

> For those of its inhabitants who rarely went beyond the parish
> boundary, the parish itself was so to speak at the centre of the
> landscape, and every place outside a point on the circumference
> of the parish, or beyond the horizon. The roads . . . were for
> them primarily an internal network, to connect different places

within the parish. For those inhabitants accustomed to moving
outside it, however, and for those travellers who passed through
it, the parish was simply one of many in a district defined not by
some circular system of geography but a linear one, as part of a
complex of roads which "intersected" each other. The topography of an open-field system was essentially the expression of the
first system, that which saw the individual place as an integral,
self-contained unit, connected as much by chance as by necessity
with other places outside it. . . . An enclosed parish was opened
out by its enclosure and made part of a much wider geographical
area.

In Goldsmith's poem at times it is as if the enclosed landscape, paradoxically in Barrell's terms, both enclosed and opened out, exposed to the
gaze and the rape of outside interests, is on the verge of participating in the
second fall of man, "While thus the land, adorned for pleasure all, / In
barren splendour feebly waits the fall" (ll. 285–86). Earlier in *The Deserted
Village* this same rhyme, with its portentous echoes of the consequences of
"man's first disobedience," had suggested the vanity and instability of post-
lapsarian happiness, and inevitable mortal and spiritual decline:

> Vain, transitory splendours! Could not all
> Reprieve the tottering mansion from its fall!
> (ll. 237–38)

The vertical movement of sin and fate, relentlessly bearing downwards
towards destruction, later takes on a more sardonic note, with a grim pun
in the following couplet:

> Here, while the proud their long-drawn pomps display,
> There the black gibbet glooms beside the way.
> (ll. 317–18)

which leads one to reflect that there is more than one way of being "long-
drawn," one certainly more painful and conclusive than any of the others,
although Goldsmith no doubt intends to press the judgment that there is not
much to choose between them, morally speaking. The gibbet overshadows
the pompous show of the proud, both figuratively and literally, a vertical
memento mori for the arrogant and the improvident along the very roads
where "the rattling chariots" rush them to their hazardous pleasures. This
whole scene is in effect an allegorical representation of the Rake's Progress.

It is no surprise, therefore, that the fiercely hostile nature of the American wilderness should be expressed partly in the vertical movements of the

blazing sun's "downward ray," where the epithet would be unnecessary but for the gathering connotations of the word. The "intolerable day" is "shed," and bats hang in "drowsy clusters": details and diction chosen for their support of the basic underlying image of the bounded group being struck from above and below in such a way as to scatter them to their doom. Tigers are waiting to spring up and down on their prey, and a tornado is preparing to blot out the usual horizontal division between land and sky (ll. 347–58).

In the final paragraphs of the poem the downward movement becomes increasingly explicit: "Kingdoms . . . to sickly greatness grown, / Boast of a florid vigour not their own" until "sapped their strength, and every part unsound, / Down, down they sink, and spread a ruin round" (ll. 393–94; cf. ll. 351–52, where a combination of vertical imagery ["Those poisonous fields with rank luxuriance *crowned*": italics added] and the horizontal ["Where the dark scorpion gathers death around"] indicates a deadly threat. The vertical energies either gather or spread death and destruction within the doomed circle). This is picked up a few lines later with the description of "the rural virtues," like protective magical powers squeezed out of the deflated body politic, vacating the land:

> Down where yon anchoring vessel spreads the sail,
> That idly waiting flaps with every gale,
> Downward they move, a melancholy band,
> Pass from the shore and darken all the strand.
>
> (ll. 399–402)

But the most complex as well as the most poignant instance of this vertical movement comes earlier, where the ascent is, paradoxically, a plethoric response to weakness and decay:

> But verging to decline, its splendours rise,
> Its vistas strike, its palaces surprise;
> While scourges by famine from the smiling land,
> The mournful peasant leads his humble band.
>
> (ll. 297–300)

This is the third occasion within less than a hundred lines that Goldsmith has described splendours that have risen but to fall; here it is suggested in a particularly hostile manner, since the secondary sense of "strike" and "surprise" imply hostile and animate presences rearing themselves among and out of the imminent ruin of the landscape, and scouring the peasantry. The climax comes in the following couplet, in which the expulsion of the native inhabitants is shown as short-circuiting the normally productive life cycle of the country, the community and the individual:

> And while he sinks, without one arm to save,
> The country blooms—a garden and a grave.
>
> (ll. 301–2)

The last line, while implying assent to the Augustan claim voiced by Pope that " 'tis Use alone that sanctifies expense" ("Epistle to Burlington"), bitterly challenges the whole tradition of the fertile garden from Chaucer to Spenser's "Garden of Adonis" ("the first seminary / Of all things that are borne to live and dye, / According to their kynde") and the Garden of Eden in *Paradise Lost*. Goldsmith suggests that a country landscape filled with flowers instead of crops resembles a cemetery, that garden in which life only exists to give a decorative trimming to the substances of decay. A nightmare impression of a phosphorescent glow plays like an artificial flame across these lines in which the bright land swallows up living men.

Alexander Pope had been able to look forward to a time when fashionable vanity, although it entertained its guests "in plenty starving, tantaliz'd in state," would be submerged beneath the tide of natural fecundity, when:

> Another age shall see the golden Ear
> Imbrown the Slope, and nod on the Parterre,
> Deep Harvest bury all his pride had plann'd,
> And laughing Ceres re-assume the land.

And even before that vision had been fulfilled, Pope was ready to acknowledge the beneficent economic contribution made by aristocratic "charitable Vanity" by which "the Poor are cloath'd, the Hungry fed; / Health to himself, and to his Infants bread / The Lab'rer bears" ("Epistle to Burlington"). It was even more true in Goldsmith's day that the greed of the powerful and the rich brought benefits to the population as a whole, as well as losses and pains; since it was only by enclosure and the economic and agricultural developments the poet deplores that the population of Britain, which during the sixty-year reign of George III doubled from about seven million to fourteen million, was able to survive. Goldsmith, not able to embrace the practical though visionary realism of Pope, nor able to "reprieve the tottering mansion from its fall," since a man is inevitably doomed by time, was by virtue of his period and his temperament prevented from finding in his painful awareness of "vain transitory splendours" Wordsworth's "strength in what remains behind":

In the primal sympathy
Which having been must ever be,
In the soothing thoughts that spring
Out of human suffering,
In the faith that looks through death,
In years that bring the philosophic mind.
      ("Ode: Intimations of Immortality,"
      ll. 183–89)

Goldsmith was not ready to believe that the solution to his anxieties, besides which Wordsworth's response to loss, at least in these lines, appears to be complacently accommodating, was to be found through introspection or in any kind of solipsistic contentment. He looked for economic or political explanations which if correct should provide a practical remedy. This may have been a deceptive way out that was historically unjustified, but it did offer him concepts and metaphors, as well as a narrative structure, with which to express his sense of loss and abandonment. Although he was not able to anticipate Wordsworth, at least in one couplet (ll. 301–2) he does seem to have looked forward to the mordant humour of another Irish exile and wanderer nearly two centuries later, who has two of his rootless and increasingly derelict emigrants consider the paradox of man's brief existence. Samuel Beckett's Pozzo laments that "they give birth astride of a grave, the light gleams an instant, then it's night once more," which leads to Vladimir's reflection a few moments later: "Astride of a grave and a difficult birth. Down in the hole, lingeringly, the grave-digger puts on the forceps. We have time to grow old. The air is full of our cries" (*Waiting for Godot*). It is more than an echo in that "lingeringly" that ties Beckett and his theatrical personae to Goldsmith and Milton; for his work like *The Deserted Village* is a perpetual reminder that "so near grows death to life."

PAT ROGERS

The Dialectic of The Traveller

In a story by Jorge Luis Borges called *El Aleph*, the narrator alludes to the manifestations of the topographic urge in literature. He observes that he once had occasion to examine the fifteen thousand Alexandrines ("dodecasílabos") which constitute Drayton's *Poly Olbion*. He terms the poem a considerable, if limited, achievement, and describes it as a less wearisome undertaking than an allied venture by Carlos Argentino:

> He had it in mind to versify the whole wide world. . . . By 1941, he had already dispatched a few hectares of the state of Queensland, rather more than a kilometre of the course of the Ob, a gasometer in the north of Veracruz, the principal business houses in the parish of Concepción, the mansion of Moriana Cambaceres de Alvear in September the Eleventh Street in Belgrano, and one of the Turkish baths not far from the celebrated aquarium in Brighton.

The passage is characteristic of Borges in its apparent literalness, its precision, and its muffled irony. One could say that the joke lies in confronting grandiose literary ambition, to provide a "comprehensive" reflection of the world, with the minuscule coverage which is all that any writer can achieve. Nevertheless, Drayton comes off relatively well, if not altogether unscathed. The absurdity of *Poly Olbion* is there on the surface, in the fifteen thousand lumbering hexameters. For its time, we feel, it was a noble enterprise; but

From *The Art of Oliver Goldsmith,* edited by Andrew Swarbrick. © 1984 by Vision Press Ltd. Barnes & Noble, 1984.

the modern world has become too complex for any such vaunting designs, so that nowadays the absurdity invades the content.

Oliver Goldsmith stood halfway between Drayton and Carlos Argentino. He wrote at a juncture when it was possible to see the inapplicability of Drayton, and yet when writers had not given up the desire to make sense of the totality of the world they inhabited. In order to survey mankind from China to Peru, it was increasingly felt as necessary that some kind of schema should be imposed on the disparate material. Indeed, the mere "survey" as such was ceasing to fulfil its task adequately. Understanding appeared to demand an argumentative structure and not just a descriptive basis. From French ideologues, above all, mid-century writers learnt to construct their anatomies of the world in terms of comparison, often in the precise guise of a dialectical system. There are the beginnings of this in James Thomson's *Liberty*; but, as I shall try to show, it is in *The Traveller* that Goldsmith evolved a fully-fledged geographical dialectic.

The main verbal activity plays around ideas which centre on *hard* and *soft*: to that extent, the poem can be related to so-called "hard" and "soft" primitivism, as those have been differentiated within the eighteenth century. The opposed notions cover many direct antitheses:

> These rocks, by custom, turn to beds of down.
> (l. 86)

> With secret course, which no loud storms annoy,
> Glides the smooth current of domestic joy.
> (ll. 433–34)

These ideas fan out to a wider contrast, between peace, ease, opulence, plenty, as against tumult, penury, deprivation. It is important that social or economic conditions as well as bare geographic or climatic facts may be involved. Indeed, part of the rhetoric of *The Traveller* is designed to equate, or at least align, these different senses of hard and soft.

But there are at least two significant complications, which are related to contemporary sensibility. First, the argumentative structure is overlaid by traditional ideas of cultural differentiation, and specifically by the new overtones of an old dichotomy—that between north and south. Secondly, the stock attributes of the seasons are hinted at, in the central sections of the poem, thus enabling Goldsmith to reinforce national stereotypes with contrasts drawn from the natural order (and thus to make them stick more firmly).

I

The distinction between the hard north and the soft south is very old and very widely spread. As far as Europe goes, it is clearly apparent in the implied contrast Tacitus draws between the virtuous Germanic tribes and the effete Romans. In many uses, the line is drawn around the Alps, with the show of limp effeminacy opening in Venice. The precise placing of the line might vary, but this broad categorization survived for centuries. It was, however, in the wake of the Enlightenment that the values of the "primitive" north could be most strategically opposed to those of the "degenerate" south; the rise of Saxon scholarship, the new interest in Nordic folklore, the emphasis on remote embattled bards (far from the Mediterranean seed-bed of high European culture), all came to the support of this strategy. For Goethe and Madame de Staël, the journey to Italy is symbolic of a shift in feeling. Mme. de Staël in Germany picks up the internal north/south distinction which is drawn in most European countries, but even southern Germany is not really "southern" in the cultural sense:

> L'Allemagne offre encore quelques traces d'une nature non habitée. Depuis les Alpes jusqu'à la mer, entre le Rhin et le Danube, vous voyez un pays couvert de chênes et de sapins, traversé par des fleuves d'une imposante beauté, et coupé par des montagnes dont l'aspect est très pittoresque; mais de vastes bruyères, des sables, des routes souvent négligées, un climat sévère, remplissent d'abord l'âme de tristesse; et ce n'est qu'à la longue qu'on découvre ce qui peut attacher à ce séjour.
>
> Le midi de l'allemagne est très bien cultivé; cependant il y a toujours dans les plus belles contrées de ce pays quelque chose de sérieux, qui fait plutôt penser au travail qu'aux plaisirs, aux vertus des habitants qu'aux charmes de la nature.
>
> (*De la Littérature: De l'Allemagne*)

When Goldsmith wrote, the precise literary implications which Mme. de Staël had in mind were not yet abroad in English culture. Nonetheless, *The Traveller* is an important stage in, as it were, unspecifying the cultural meaning of north and south, and thus making the distinction available as part of a general critique.

Modern geopolitics has reasserted the biblical potency of east and west. But for many centuries it was north and south which seemed the central divide. When an image of absolute contrariety was needed, it was frequently

to this notion that writers turned: witness Richard, Duke of York, to the
Queen in *3 Henry VI*:

> Thou art as opposite to every good
> As the Antipodes are unto us,
> Or as the south to the septentrion.
>
> (1.4.136)

The epithets associated with these points of the compass, signifying "characteristic of the north [south]," came to have definite associations, which
may be tracked down in *O.E.D.* citations. Thus Pope in the *Essay on
Criticism:*

> Which not alone the *Southern Wit* sublimes,
> But ripens Spirits in cold *Northern Climes.*

Indeed, without any direct mention of climatic factors, the terms brought
with them strong implications, so that "northern" by itself might suggest
the "cold Septentrion blasts" of *Paradise Regained.* Moreover, as interest in
the Gothic developed, both in the area of political theory and of linguistic
inquiry, the associations of "northern" acquired a new penumbra, as (by
implied absence) did those of its antonym. Many of these tendencies, already hinted at in a writer like Sir William Temple, become acutely present
in Montesquieu, notably book 1 of *L'Esprit des lois,* chapters 14–17. Chapter 14 asserts some of the commonplaces passed down to the Enlightenment: "people of the North are less capable of [pain] than the delicate fibre
of the inhabitants of warm countries. . . . You must flay a Muscovite alive to
make him feel." A Muscovite, note, is culturally a northerner; the term
connotes a climatic region and a cultural grouping, not a precise geographic
area.

The second standard system which is exploited in *The Traveller* is
related in some ways. This is the lore of the seasons, as transmitted through
poetry, painting and music. Each season had acquired its own set of attributes, which were commonly employed to define and characterize the
particular stage in a yearly cycle. In recent English poetry, two works which
contributed powerfully to the tradition were Pope's *Pastorals* and Thomson's
Seasons; both had given the traditional motifs a new imaginative direction.
Today an even more familiar creation produced in this line of artistic thought
is the set of concerti by Vivaldi, known collectively as *Le Stagione*; each of
the individual items has a sonnet describing the setting and events in terms
of the stock seasonal associations. Some of these properties, I shall argue,

were borrowed by Goldsmith to enforce his rhetoric of modal contrast and psychological differentiation.

We do not know as much as we might wish about the intellectual genesis of the poem. The dedication to Oliver's brother Henry contains one brief paragraph of some interest, on the fortunes of the different art-forms as civilization expands; but otherwise this is a document of moderate value. The poet's scanty collection of letters does not provide a single reference to *The Traveller* (a single apparent exception occurs in a letter now shown to have been a forgery). The sale catalogue of Goldsmith's library, conveniently reprinted in the Mansell series, does at least permit one to confine one's guesswork regarding influences within a decently measurable span. But of course mere possession of a volume can never by itself be taken to prove familiarity or even bare acquaintance. Nevertheless, this is one of the areas of evidence I shall be drawing on in my account of the poem, along with a slightly less dangerous source—that is, the books cited or alluded to in Goldsmith's published writings (principally, of course, those written prior to *The Traveller*). The parallels noted by previous editors—Dobson, Friedman, Dixon, Lonsdale and others—are incorporated where they bear directly on my case. In checking the contemporary meaning of key terms in Johnson's *Dictionary*, one occasionally encounters illustrative passages which help to draw the intellectual boundaries of Goldsmith's undertaking. These, then, are some of the main aids to my inquiry.

A word should be perhaps added on the previous readings of this poem, and the relation of my essay to them. The critical heritage is disappointingly thin. G. S. Rousseau's collection shows that a fair amount of attention was devoted to the work in the century following its composition. Indeed, this particular volume of the Critical Heritage series opens with Johnson's famous assessment in the *Critical Review* for December 1764. Nothing else reproduced by Rousseau is much more help than Johnson's account, brief and generalized though it is. John Langhorne in the *Monthly Review* is fuller but scarcely more detailed in his commentary. Among the later items, Dr. John Aikin provides a fairly intelligent paraphrase, whilst Leigh Hunt has some provocative thoughts on the "metrical weakness" of the poem: "GOLDSMITH in his *Traveller* is feeble in misplaced emphasis; for his words are of sufficient length and sound to be pompous in a better situation: he slides now and then into a kind of hurried halt, which is as lame as the feebleness of monosyllables." But the most important contribution is certainly that of the biographer Prior, who offers much more concrete and substantive analysis. He suggests Addison's *Letter from Italy* as a model; he conducts a detailed investigation into Goldsmith's revisions of the text; and, most important, he provides what is still the best comparison with *Childe Harold*, surely a genuine historical conjuncture rather than an arbitrary collision momentarily engineered by dreams of intertextualism.

Later criticism has likewise owed a good deal to biographers. William Black's volume in the English Men of Letters series (1878) devotes a not very illuminating chapter to the poem. But Austin Dobson in his study (1888) is, predictably, more lively and historically aware, whilst John Forster's life of Goldsmith (1848), although drawing heavily on Prior, makes a significant independent contribution (I do not altogether share Rousseau's estimate of the relative merit of these biographies). In the twentieth century Ralph M. Wardle has written much the best of the lives, and his comments on *The Traveller*, if tending towards faint praise, contain some useful information. The recent critics who have engaged most fully with the poem are Robert H. Hopkins and Ricardo Quintana. The latter gives what seems to me a valuable perspective; he mentions not just Addison but also *Cooper's Hill* and *Windsor Forest*. His conclusion is this:

> *The Traveller* is prospect poetry literally and figuratively; it is a series of verse *characters*, by means of which the different national cultures of the west are compared; it is a patriotic poem, though the patriotism is of a different order from the uncritical nationalism of Addison's *Letter*, it is an estimate of contemporary conditions, condemning much but finding consolation in the thought that nature and reason afford mankind a moral mean between deplorable extremities.

Hopkins sees in the poem an "antithesis of centripetal and centrifugal patterns," more widely a conflict between action and motion. I shall not be pursuing these notions, but Quinatana's phrase regarding "verse characters" is pertinent to my theme (as is a good deal of Lonsdale's introductory comment). The question is: *how* does Goldsmith characterize the different cultures, and what modes of typing (social, political, psychological) are utilized in the effort?

II

In chapter 13 of his *Enquiry into the Present State of Polite Learning in Europe*, Goldsmith touched on an important matter of presentation:

> COUNTRIES wear very different appearances to travellers of different circumstances. A man who is whirled through Europe in

a post chaise, and the pilgrim who walks the grand tour on foot,
will form very different conclusions.
   Haud inexpertus loquor.

The implications of this statement for literary travellers were being explored
at this very juncture by Sterne, and soon Smollett was also to face them. As
far as Goldsmith's poem is concerned, he takes the bold step of dispensing
with the ordinary "progress" framework altogether. By placing his narrator
on his aerial vantage point, the poet eliminates the need to mimic a physical
journey from one country to another. The observer, set "on high above the
storm's career" (l. 33), possesses a kind of simultaneous visual and moral
grasp of all Europe, unaffected by local accidents of weather. The advantage
is that his perceptual and conceptual view can seem a panorama achieved at
a glance. The necessary transitions involve a "turn" of the gaze (l. 165), not
a perambulation of the body. As a result, his judgements seem less subjective, less dependent on the mode of entry. His outlook is spatial, detemporal-
ized; in McLuhan's terms, one might almost say, the narrator achieves the
instantaneous reception of messages found in electronic rather than printed
means of communication. Putting the matter in more guarded historical
terms, one could say that Goldsmith is clinging on to the quasi-impersonality
of the epic formula at a time when most of the newer tendencies in literature—in the novel, above all—were working in the opposite direction.
   What this means, when we come to the review of the individual countries, is that the traveller escapes just those rigours of passage which constitute so much of the ordinary fare of eighteenth-century travel writing. He
is, so to speak, disembodied. Although the opening of the poem tells us of
his aimless journeys about the globe, and of his disconsolate verdict that he
can call "no spot of all the world [his] own" (l. 30), once he achieves his
eyrie above the Alps, his posture is static. He is *sitting*, we must always
remember, throughout his survey of Europe. As distinct from the traditional
vagabond, he sees most when he stops still. Unlike Cain, or the Wandering
Jew, or the Ancient Mariner, or the Flying Dutchman, this traveller is al-
lowed, if not to rest, at least to escape his curse long enough to take stock
of the places he has visited. His "pensive hour" is spent not in analysing his
own experiences, but in reaching fresh conclusions. The poem represents a
release from obsession, as "The Ancient Mariner" does not. This is all very
different from, for example, Savage's poem *The Wanderer* (1729), a possible distant model for Goldsmith. Savage describes his poem as "a vision,"
and indeed his narrator achieves only glimpses of insight. Despite his invo-
cation of

> CONTEMPLATION, whose unbounded Gaze,
> Swift in a Glance, the Course of Things, surveys;
> Who in *Thy-self* the various View can'st find
> Of Sea, Land, Air, and Heav'n, and human Kind.

Savage does not attain any stable perspective on events. There appears to be some arcane, perhaps Masonic, message; the ultimate drift of the poem is closer to that of *The Magic Flute* than that of any other work which comes to mind. And Savage's wanderer does wander: that is to say, his movements are jerky, charted only imprecisely, seemingly unplanned. On the other hand, Goldsmith's traveller carries out a logical, almost abstract survey of major western countries. There is no attempt to dramatize the sheer *confusion* which is so often the lot of the traveller on the ground. Why should there be? He is, explicitly and intentionally, not "on the ground."

What has happened, crucially, is that the philosophic traveller has done more than travel; he has studied philosophy. It is at this point that Goldsmith's reading becomes relevant. By this I mean not so much his stock of orthodox travel books, to which the sale catalogue unsurprisingly testifies. Rather, we should look to the works on social, political and constitutional theory; the historical tomes which dealt with such matters as the fall of empires; the treatments of large cultural debates such as the *querelle* of Ancients and Moderns. In the library catalogue, we do indeed find represented authors such as Puffendorf; Charles Rollin; Bossuet; Vertot; Père d'Orleans; Fontenelle; Sir William Temple (four volumes), and so on. The dates of the editions are not always cited, but all those named could have been in Goldsmith's possession in 1760. That comment does not apply to other items, which herald the arrival of the Enlightenment: Diderot's *Oeuvres*, in five volumes, or Helvétius's *De l'Homme*. The only Rousseau represented is a collection of 1734 which obviously derives from the poet Jean-Baptiste. More intriguing is the set of Voltaire in nineteen odd volumes: when they were acquired it is impossible to guess, though the *Memoirs of M. de Voltaire* indicate that Goldsmith might have had a need for such a thing by 1759. Almost equally intriguing is item 7 among the octavos, "Voyage par Winckelman." But these are speculative connections, and it is more appropriate to consider one firm link.

This concerns Montesquieu, who appears twice in the sale catalogue. Item 4 among the smaller books is "Lettres de Montesquieu"; item 89 is "Montesquieu on the Roman Empire, 1759." There can be no doubt about the latter entry: it concerns *Considérations sur les causes de la grandeur des Romains et de leur décadence* (1734). This was translated as *Reflections . . .*

in the same year, and an edition appeared in London in 1759. There is, naturally, no guarantee that Goldsmith actually obtained it in that year: but it is altogether probable. As for the other item, that must surely refer to the *Lettres Persanes*, though in which of the numerous editions it is impossible to say. A further piece of evidence is found among John Newbery's papers, as cited by Forster. These show that Goldsmith borrowed a number of books in November 1762, for compilation purposes: these included "*Encyclopediae [sic]*, 8 vols., French; *Chinese Letters*, French; *Persian* Do." We also know that in August 1757 Goldsmith had written for the *Monthly Review* an essay on Voltaire, ending with a brief discussion of Montesquieu which alludes to both the works listed in the sale catalogue. There is also an article on Montesquieu in the *Critical Review* in 1759, ascribed by Forster to Goldsmith, but not accepted into the canon by Friedman.

The glaring omission, of course, is *L'Esprit des lois*. The 1757 article just mentioned does briefly allude to the work: but a fuller reference occurs in the *Enquiry into the Present State of Polite Learning in Europe*:

> MONTESQUIEU, a name equally deserving fame with the former [Voltaire]. The Spirit of Laws is an instance, how much genius is able to lead learning. His system has been adopted by the literati; and yet is it not possible for opinions equally plausible to be formed upon opposite principles, if a genius like his, could be found to attempt such an undertaking? He seems more a poet than a philosopher.

Those familiar with Goldsmith's habits as a compiler will not be surprised to hear that this reserved judgement goes along with unacknowledged borrowings elsewhere. The importance of Montesquieu lay in something Goldsmith may not have consciously perceived. He had made the different characteristics of nations an object of philosophic survey rather than of geographical description.

This sense of abstraction is immediately apparent when, at line 63, Goldsmith begins to establish his antithetical terms (ll. 63–72):

> But where to find that happiest spot below,
> Who can direct, when all pretend to know?
> The shudd'ring tenant of the frigid zone
> Boldly proclaims that happiest spot his own,
> Extols the treasures of his stormy seas,
> And his long nights of revelry and ease;
> The naked Negro, panting at the line,

> Boasts of his golden sands and palmy wine,
> Basks in the glare, or stems the tepid wave,
> And thanks his Gods for all the good they gave.

The opposition of the "frigid zone" and equatorial regions is a traditional way of viewing the range of human existence. Here, the climatic contrast is enforced by prominent items of diction, whose conventionality prevents us from lingering too insistently on their literal import—*shudd'ring; basks; tepid* (a word given new energy by Thomson). The contrast is drawn in less sweeping, that is more specific, terms a little later (ll. 83–6):

> With food as well the peasant is supply'd
> On Idra's cliffs as Arno's shelvy side;
> And though the rocky crested summits frown,
> These rocks, by custom, turn to beds of down.

The hint of oxymoron which hovers around much of the text comes almost to the surface at such junctures. The copulative "turn" functions as not much more than an equal sign; much of the work, semantically, is thrust on the concentrated phrase "by custom" (Lonsdale is the only editor I have seen who notes the parallel with *Othello* 1.3.230–32). Behind both passages lies a body of writing which reviews human life as it is lived in extreme conditions. *The Seasons* was, of course, a classic treatment of both tropics and arctic regions; and as McKillop has shown in his own classic treatment [*The Background of Thomson's Seasons*], some well-thumbed sources regularly provide the material for Thomson. One of the important sources was the widely popular *Spectacle de la Nature*, by the Abbé Pluche, which extended physicotheology into speculations in the field of geology, climatology and meteorology. It has been shown that Goldsmith used Pluche in compiling his *Animated Nature*. Here I wish only to add that among the items in the sale catalogue is no. 18, "Nature Displayed, 7 vol. 1757." This can be identified as a translation of *La Spectacle de la Nature* which went through several editions in the middle of the century.

There follows a passage meditating on such abstractions as art, "Wealth, commerce, honour, liberty, content," all typical elements in the cultural debate in which Montesquieu is such a seminal figure. However, it is when we reach the direct application to Italy that Goldsmith's language most insistently plays around the physical and moral terminology used in this debate. Italy, needless to say, is connected with "soft" values. We must recall that until the Hellenistic revival of the romantic era, British attitudes towards Mediterranean countries tended to carry many double-edged associations. Goldsmith never uses the simple word "luxury," that is the noun (although "luxuriance" and "luxurious" occur); nevertheless, the central unstated subject could be expressed by that word. And underlying the passage is the belief that ancient Rome had endured harsher winters than modern Italy, with a consequent effect on the nature of the inhabitants. This view is expressed in an essay ascribed to Goldsmith by R. S. Crane, which appeared in May 1760 under the title "The Effect which Climates have upon Man." The writer describes the climatic shift, and continues: "Need we then be at such a loss to account for the different manners of the ancient Romans and modern Italians? a warm country ever producing an effeminacy of manners among the inhabitants." *Effeminacy* is a rich concept, historically; its main thrust here is in the direction of the spineless and effete Latins, but the idea of self-indulgence includes a possible notion of sexual over-activity (heterosexual, in fact: a strange lexical component as the word is used today).

The vocabulary expressing this view of Italy is built around terms such as *bounty, blooms, torrid, blossom, smiling.* It is, indeed, the precise lexicon appropriated to summer in the standard seasonal division. Several of the key words actually turn up in Thomson's *Summer* (*blooms, torrid, luxurious, bliss, gelid, grove, bright, smiling,* etc.). One might even say that Goldsmith has simply made explicit the political meanings inherent in Thomson's natural order, where "all-conquering Heat" and "the powerful King of Day" suggest a potency extending beyond generative force into a sort of absolutism and tyranny. Inevitably, some of the parallels recall other parts of Thomson's poem: "the varied year" (l. 116) suggests the opening line of *Winter*. However, the congruence is far more pervasive and marked in the case of *Summer*. Italy is the traditional south, that is a profuse and glaring landscape, inducing laziness and lack of moral fibre. It is equally summer transformed into a socio-political phenomenon.

Goldsmith then makes a full turn (the verbal gesture indicating a geographical shift, but also a switch in poetic attitude); his next subject is defined thus (ll. 165–68):

> turn we to survey
> Where rougher climes a nobler race display,
> Where the bleak Swiss their stormy mansions tread,
> And force a churlish soil for scanty bread.

"Bleak" as applied to the Swiss might be taken as a transferred epithet, referring primarily to the setting in which their lives are lived out. However, it is impossible to be positive on such a point, since the technique blurs any notion of transference. The people themselves partake of the quality of their landscape (ll. 169–70):

> No product here the barren hills afford,
> But man and steel, the soldier and his sword.

Again, there are close affinities to the language used by Thomson in *The Seasons*. But this time *Winter* is the relevant section, even though Thomson does not have much to say about the Alps as such. (His treatment of Savoy describes the effect on "the happy *Grisons*" when an avalanche destroys their settlements.) Both poems relate "the Rigours of the Year" (*Winter*, l. 424) to deprivation, barren wastes, scanty living. Words common to the vocabulary of the two poets include *storm, gloom, chill, torrent, roar* (of wind and sea), *want* (noun), *struggle, scanty, humble, calm, bleak, keen,* and so on—sternness and severity are imputed to both climate and personality. Thomson writes explicitly about the northern landscapes; Goldsmith borrows some of the standard terms to characterize the Swiss.

In addition, this is one of the places in *The Traveller* where the connection with Montesquieu becomes quite explicit. Goldsmith describes the "level life" of the hardy Swiss mountain people, "unfit for raptures," and sets out in sharply schematic terms the "coarseness" of their moral being (ll. 227–38):

> But not their joys alone thus coarsly flow:
> Their morals, like their pleasures, are but low.
> For, as refinement stops, from sire to son
> Unalter'd, unimprov'd the manners run,
> And love and friendship's finely pointed dart
> Fall blunted from each indurated heart.
> Some sterner virtues o'er the mountain's breast
> May sit, like falcons cow'ring on the nest;
> But all the gentler morals, such as play
> Through life's more cultur'd walks, and charm the way,
> These far dispers'd, on timorous pinions fly,
> To sport and flutter in a kinder sky.

There is some individuality in the expression here, as with the simile of the falcons. But the root concepts can all be traced in *L'Esprit des lois,* notably in book 14; I cite the contemporary translation by Thomas Nugent, which Goldsmith is exceedingly likely to have known, although the modern version by Melvin Richter sometimes approaches more closely to the poet's vocabulary.

> In cold countries they have very little sensibility for pleasure. . . .
> The large bodies and coarse fibres of the people of the North are
> less capable of laceration than the delicate fibres of the inhabit-
> ants of warm countries. . . . In northern regions a machine ro-
> bust and heavy finds pleasure in whatever is apt to throw the
> spirits into motion, such as hunting, travelling, war, and wine. If
> we travel towards the North, we meet with people who have few
> vices, many virtues, and a great share of frankness and sincerity.

The wants of the Swiss are "few," their "barren" state is devoid of any
"pleasing science." Their course of life is "unfann'd by strong desire." This
is pretty well identical with Montesquieu's view of the culture of northern
countries, where "imagination, taste, sensibility, and vivacity" are far less in
evidence (along with vice) than in southern climes. Goldsmith makes little
effort to differentiate his theme from that of Montesquieu, except perhaps
insofar as his reference to patriotism (l. 199ff.) may allude to a long-
celebrated national characteristic among the Swiss cantons. Otherwise, the
contrast between penurious virtue and self-indulgent opulence (the point of
setting Switzerland against Italy) is in essence a development of
Montesquieu's typology of northern and southern races.

Another "turn" is dramatized at line 239, with France the new centre
of attention. This would seem to belong, in strict climatology, to
Montesquieu's intermediate category of the "temperate." If anything, however, Goldsmith aligns it with the warm-blooded side of his scheme: though
warmth is secondary here to light and movement. In fact, this "Gay sprightly
land of mirth and social ease" is characterized very much in terms of the
seasonal properties attached to spring. The opening line itself, "To kinder
skies, where gentler manners reign," echoes the very start of Thomson's
Spring: "Come, gentle Spring, Etherial Mildness, come." Again we find an
unmistakable convergence of idiom as between *The Seasons* and *The Traveller*, manifest above all in the words which relate to stock properties of
spring: *soft* (the crucial single expression), *gay, zephyr, freshen, busy, maze,
kind, sportive*. Thomson celebrates "the Symphony of Spring," and Goldsmith takes over the musical imagery of the earlier poet (*choir, murmur*); in
fact, the traveller piping inexpertly for the dancers supplies a comic replay
of the pastoral Golden Age of *Spring*, lines 267ff. ("For Music held the
whole in perfect Peace"). "Dance and Sport" are common themes: but the
double-edged "social ease" of *The Traveller* has its source, too, in *Spring*,
with "Luxury and Ease." The epithet *social* occurs on another occasion in
Goldsmith's short passage: this echoes several key usages in Thomson, where

"social Feeling" is a key to humanity and understanding of nature. Thomson writes of "the Spirit of the genial Year," and a whole cluster of ramified associations spill out from "genial"—parents and children, love, festivity, hospitality, creativity. Goldsmith has much less space and a less complex rhetoric, but he too evokes psychological states by means of seasonal motifs. In his dialectic the French have become too soft, too vain and ostentatious: this is the obverse of their civility and charm. Even Montesquieu had picked out "the vanity of a Frenchman" as contributing to the energy of the race— his point is taken from Mandeville, that is the idea that vanity, unlike pride, in "encouraging a trifling turn of mind" serves to increase commercial activity. Although Goldsmith lays his emphasis elsewhere, he draws on the same set of national stereotypes.

Finally in this tetrad (a very common and characteristic formal layout in Augustan literature) comes Holland. Once again the very opening state-ment incorporates hints of the seasonal lore: "To men of other minds my fancy flies, / Embosom'd in the deep where Holland lies" (ll. 281–82). The proleptic hint of Keats's great ode is not wholly fortuitous; Thomson, too, had lit on the expression "in thy Bosom grow" in the first fifteen lines of *Autumn*, and the significant epithet occurs in expressions such as "deep-loaded Bough" later in his poem. Goldsmith's lines continue with a number of the terms consecrated to autumn, with *treasure, wealth, gain, cultivated, toil,* amongst others. The argument here is that "Convenience, plenty, ele-gance, and arts" have been perverted by the greed of the people; uncorrupted, these were the traditional benefits of a prosperous harvest. At the heart of Thomson's poem is a celebration of the blessings of industry (ll. 44–6):

> Whom Labour still attends, and Sweat, and Pain;
> Yet the kind Source of every gentle Art,
> And all the soft Civility of Life.

Goldsmith refers to "repeated toil, / Industrious habits [which] in each bos-om reign, / And industry begets a love of gain." There is a stronger sense than elsewhere of the land itself, "the wave-subjected soil"; traditionally autumn was associated with the element of earth, and agricultural rather than broadly pastoral activities were emphasized. Once again Goldsmith forges a negative critique by converting the usual terms of praise to a hostile end; the "treasures" of autumn, as celebrated along expected lines by Thomson, have become baneful emblems of a nation's greed. The Dutch are seen as "dull," slow, crafty, hard-hearted. The "yellow blossom'd vale" no longer connotes laughing Ceres; it links, as the passage develops and opens out imagistically, with the lure of gold. The stagnation of natural feeling among the people derives from a kind of national log-jam, a plethora of commercial bustle. Some of the flatness of the landscape and the temperance of the climate has leaked through into the national character.

After this repeated pattern of thesis and antithesis—soft, hard, soft, hard—comes the synthesis. Britain occupies the place which Thomson allots to his concluding hymn in *The Seasons*; and though Goldsmith gives disproportionate space to this section—aesthetically, as well as structurally— he does not achieve such a convincing resolution. Britain is clearly temperate, spring-like, but not enfeebled by social frivolity as France is. The poet uses superlative forms of the semantically moderate epithets that go with these attributes of temperance: "the gentlest breezes," "Creation's mildest charms." The imagery of wheels and the motions of a system (ll. 347–48) is strongly suggestive of Montesquieu; the "ferments" and "factions" are those of a free people, not just as Goldsmith sees it, but in the terms Montesquieu had used to analyse British constitution in books 11 and 19 of *L'Esprit des lois*. In this final section, too, we encounter renewed use of oxymoron (see ll. 398, 400); the contrasts hinge on ideas of excessive hardness and softness, northern and southern attributes as the poetry has defined these: for have we not (ll. 401–4)

> Seen opulence, her grandeur to maintain,
> Lead stern depopulation in her train,
> And over fields, where scatter'd hamlets rose,
> In barren solitary pomp repose?

The opposites which had been played one against another, earlier on in the text, are now thrust together to concentrate the energies of the cultural argument in a single image. It is Britain's mission, so the rhetoric would insist, to steer a middle course between despotism and anarchy, between excessive independence and excessive absorption in "social" living, between rigour and indulgence. What Montesquieu had set out as a model for the purposes of political explanation, Goldsmith has idealized into a sort of cultural myth. Unlike Carlos Argentino, he has given his survey of the "civilised" world a shape unrelated to mere topographic connections. *The Traveller* is a reading of contemporary society, sentimental in its ultimate pieties perhaps, but as a poetic argument solid and coherent in construction.

BERNARD HARRIS

She Stoops to Conquer

It is peculiarly senseless to attempt to analyse comedy. Tragedy is concerned with death, and necessitates judgement. But comedy depends upon the temporary postponement of disaster, and is concerned with the momentary, not the inevitable. There is no limit to the platitudes which such study may invoke. Johnson recognized this when composing a prologue for a failed comedy by Hugh Kelly, *A Word to the Wise,* for a benefit show on behalf of Kelly's widow and children:

> To wit, reviving from its author's dust,
> Be kind, ye judges, or at least be just. . . .
> Let one great payment every claim appease,
> And him who cannot hurt, allow to please;
> To please by scenes, unconscious of offence,
> By harmless merriment, or useful sense. . . .
> If want of skill or want of care appear,
> Forbear to hiss;—the poet cannot hear.
> By all, like him, must praise and blame be found,
> At last, a fleeting gleam, or empty sound.

Johnson's habitual melancholy was not in evidence on the occasion of Goldsmith's triumph, but the difference between success and disaster is marginal. Goldsmith was adroit enough to see the complications which the support of his powerful friends had posed for him. He was exposed to their innu-

From *The Art of Oliver Goldsmith*, edited by Andrew Swarbrick. © 1984 by Vision Press Ltd. Barnes & Noble, 1984.

endo—he was poisoning himself by wrong prescription—but like the true
gambler he put himself at risk, and hazarded all.

The plot of *She Stoops to Conquer* is simple in action, however complex in origin. Susan Hamlyn reminds us that it depends "on the device of
sending Marlow and Hastings to the House of Marlow's intended father-
in-law, a place where he would naturally wish to display his best behaviour,
on the pretence that it is an inn." She offers a fresh suggestion for yet
another source, a jest from *Quick's Whim*:

> A sailor, half-groggy, passing along the street of a certain seaport
> town, discovered over an admiral's door an escutcheon, and very
> naturally took it for an ale-house—the gentleman (a ruddy look-
> ing portly man) standing at the door, he clapped him on the
> shoulder, *Damn it, landlord, you look like an honest fellow, give
> us a cup of the best.*—The gentleman, to carry on the joke,
> ordered his servants to bring him some beer, which being done,
> the jolly tar drank towards the landlord's good health, and en-
> quired what was to pay, which the officer told him he might
> settle the next time he came that way.

Hamlyn's proposal is initially attractive, mainly because of the connection
with Quick. But his book was published more than twenty years after the
performance of the play, and may represent not a source but a defeated
memory and a vulgarized intelligence. The sources of *She Stoops to Conquer* are legion and are certainly not contained in this slight anecdote. It is
richness of allusion, not confinement of anecdote, which endows the play,
already robust with references which have escaped successive editors, with
popular acceptance. The story which Goldsmith's sister told, that he lodged
at the house of a friend in the mistaken belief that it was an inn, has the
benefit that it is more associated with folk-lore than a drunken sailor's
anecdote. And Goldsmith was drawing on deeper sources that Quick's quips.
That the dramatist "never alluded to this legend and has left no clues as to
its authenticity" is no argument. Goldsmith never alluded to a great many
matters about which we would wish to have confirmation. As Hamlyn
admits of her preferred source, "authoritative proof that Goldsmith used
this, or, indeed, any of them has not been found and is likely to remain
elusive." Goldsmith was always elusive. He was in pursuit of larger matters
that great comedy encompasses, not simply farce which diminishes response
by hurried manipulation.

The subtitle, "The mistakes of a night," is an obvious and provocative
allusion to *A Midsummer Night's Dream*. But Goldsmith was usually more

subtle than even his friends supposed. Here he challenged them to make comparison with the only writer Garrick acknowledged, and though Goldsmith managed to comply with the taste of his age, he also subverted some of its assumptions about class, choice in life, and notions of independence. The eventual title, *She Stoops to Conquer,* was chosen late, but brings with it overtones which we would be stupid to ignore:

> Kneel down and take my blessing, good my girl.
> Wilt thou not stoop?

> You did know
> How much you were my conqueror.

> And can shee, who no longer would be shee,
> Being such a Tabernacle, stoop to be
> In paper wrapt; or, when shee would not lie,
> In such a house, dwell in an Elegie?

The play is haunted by such literary reminiscences, most too familiar to mention, and also by infusions of Irish interest which defy editors, and may be self-indulgent, but never intrude upon the enjoyment of audiences or readers. Goldsmith was writing, in a manner both calculating and inspired, a prose comedy of ideal, romantic love. To do this he needed to create a fresh dialogue, compounded of his own experience, and one which Shakespeare and Vanbrugh had already accomplished, in their own time, and in their own way. They wrote comedies about love, in which the equality of men and women was recognized, whatever expedients were made necessary by social or stage conventions. Deprived of Shakespeare's opportunity to entrust so much emotional charge to the substitution of role to boy-players, Goldsmith found a new release: feminine energies would rely on deception, like the basic plot of the play.

Goldsmith had learned from the criticism of *The Good Natur'd Man* to simplify his plot. From the basic misunderstanding of a country house for an inn derive multiple related misunderstandings; Sheridan Morley [writing in *Punch*] calls the plot "the British theatre's first example of a truly triumphant running gag." In addition to a situation which any audience, even the first one, could grasp immediately, he had also sharpened his style from the convoluted manner of his first play; almost the only device is antithesis, but now unlaboured. The speed of delivery enabled him not only to please an audience, but to divert them from their prejudices. Thus by setting the action in an "old-fashioned" country house, with servants named Diggory and Pimple, visited by fashionable society intent on despising a household whose ridiculous mistress admits that she has never once been to London and derives her notion of fashion from journals, Goldsmith indulges his audience's prejudices, but contrives their discomfort, as with the characters, when the rural wits prove more than equal to the metropolitan.

Speed alone would result in farce. But *She Stoops to Conquer* is a true comedy because the dexterity of plotting reveals complicated feelings which define individuality, not stereotypes. There are reversals of an audience's expectations. Thus, mindful of the reception of the bailiffs, his "low" character is a squire of inherited social status; he is the hero, in the practical sense that he sets off the plot, and though a boisterous, hard drinking, song-making, lover of cock-fighting, horse racing man of energy and no thought, illiterate into the bargain, yet he contrives to gain his inheritance and assist the romantic lovers Constance and Hastings in getting their own inheritance and freedom. Lumpkin's sheer energy drives the play along; his vigorous rural vocabulary sets off the formal language of the lovers, though he can mimic polite and sentimental discourse (as in pretending to court Miss Neville) when it suits him to deceive his mother, on whom he takes physical revenge in the wild coach ride. By contrast, Marlow, the play's technical hero, a sophisticated womanizer, is endowed with an endearing and humiliating stammer which inhibits his stilted conversation when with a woman of his own class, but is eloquent in the presence of servants. This confusion of language and class seems to me to get to the heart of the comedy. The mistakes of the night are resolved not by Puck's magic, but by human conspiracy, in which the central agent is the heroine.

The trick by which Kate Hardcastle assumes her role of serving-girl (a device as successful as Rosalind's) is made possible not by a stage convention but the idiosyncrasy of her father who prefers her to dress as a maid in the evening. (We need not attribute sinister motives here, though St. John Hankin made a witty playlet about the subsequent married life of Kate Hardcastle and Marlow, in which she rescues their failing relationship by role-playing as a maid with cap and broom.) We should not discount unconscious forces in any comedy, but Goldsmith's interest seems more likely to be in the way parental demands, however eccentric, may be honoured by a dutiful daughter; and the false sentiment then discarded:

> *Enter* MISS HARDCASTLE, *plainly dress'd.*
> HARDCASTLE . Well, my Kate, I see you have changed your dress
>   as I bid you; and yet, I believe, there was no great occasion.
> MISS HARDCASTLE. I find such a pleasure, Sir, in obeying your

commands, that I take care to observe them without ever debating their propriety.

Such sweet submission should have warned her father that pretended sentiments are sometimes the means of obtaining one's own way. Kate's first reaction to Marlow's halting conversation is laughter:

> Was there ever such a sober sentimental interview? I'm certain he scarce look'd in my face the whole time. Yet the fellow, but for his unaccountable bashfulness, is pretty well too. He has good sense, but then so buried in his fears, that it fatigues one more than ignorance. If I could teach him a little confidence, it would be doing somebody that I know of a piece of service. But who is that somebody?—that, faith, is a question I can scarce answer.

The economy of such language, as with the previous illustration, compresses not only conflicting feelings but the activities which true dramatic language is always required to carry. There is both plot-furtherance in "he scarce looked in my face"—preparing us for Kate's questioning of her maid "are you sure he does not remember my face or person?"—and emotional dawning; there is a pun on "interview" in both scenes, and preparation in "service" for the eventual dissimulation of being a barmaid. Her question, "But who is that somebody?" is offered in coquetry to the audience, and is also one she asks herself.

It is only necessary to labour such detail because the "naturalness" of the result may make us overlook the art. The versatility of Goldsmith's language has never been denied, but the subtlety is still there in simplicity. In one way the comedy trades natural humour in place of the striving after brilliance, and the range of personal relationships is therefore wider than in more sophisticated social comedies. Lumpkin would be no more than a buffoon in such surroundings, not the anarchic principle he is here; Hastings and Miss Neville would be sentimental lovers in more genteel company, but become conspirators here, and form a foil for the more individualistic Kate; the extent to which the play explores family relationships, daughter and father, husband and wife, son and mother, is a more satisfying, fuller concept of comic relationships than in many restricted social comedies, and defies restrictions of the polite, the merely witty. It provides an order of release at various levels, for Kate, for Marlow, for Tony Lumpkin, for the young lovers; even, if harshly, for Mrs. Hardcastle. The play is very much about such liberation, and Goldsmith managed this by not directly challenging too violently the acceptance of his audience, but by subversion, and by capturing a mood in his own society so comprehensively that, in the manner of all truly successful comedy, it remains renewable and available to subsequent experiences in totally different circumstances.

THOMAS R. PRESTON

The Uses of Adversity:
Worldly Detachment
and Heavenly Treasure
in The Vicar of Wakefield

Revisionist criticism of *The Vicar of Wakefield* portrays Parson Primrose as a moral monster whom Goldsmith ridicules and holds up for the reader's contempt. Robert Hopkins, for example, claims the Vicar is an "object of satire," a clergyman whose moral "complacency is nauseous" (*The True Genius of Oliver Goldsmith*). Because the Vicar uses such terms as "benevolence now repaid with unexpected interest"; agrees with his wife's attempts to marry the girls into money; and views his children as "treasures" who "will be our support and our pleasure," the reader should view him as a pious fraud who is really a money-conscious, fortune-hunting materialist, practicing benevolence as a good business investment and treating his children as "annuities for old age." From the revisionist perspective the Vicar's "moralism is corrupted by the world of the counting house." According to Richard Jaarsma, "Essentially, Dr. Primrose is a small man, pettyminded, and, although he disavows it, very much concerned with the things of this world."

The Vicar undoubtedly receives his share of satiric attack, and usually, I think, from himself, but nowhere in the story does he emerge as the hypocritical villain the revisionists suppose. The *Vicar*, while often using the formal realism associated with the novel, does not, in the terms of [Robert] Scholes and [Robert] Kellogg, fall into the category of "representational" narrative that intends to "reproduce actuality," referring for meaning to "historical, psychological, or sociological truth" (*The Nature of Narrative*).

From *Studies in Philology* 81, no. 2 (Spring 1984). © 1984 by the University of North Carolina Press.

Its many narrative strategies, drawn from satire, the novel, the romance, the exemplary tale, and other literary forms, indicate instead an "illustrative" narrative referring for its meaning to "ethical and metaphysical truth." The Vicar's biblical diction and frequent biblical allusions, appropriate for a clergyman, suggest, in fact, an illustrative narrative that is primarily tropological, one in which characters and events imitate, recapitulate, or participate in the meaning of biblical or doctrinal characters, events, and themes to exemplify a Christian moral or truth. The proper context, then, for interpreting the *Vicar*, as both Martin Battestin and James Lehmann indicate in their important studies of the Vicar's use of Job allusions, is eighteenth-century biblical criticism, primarily the hermeneutic writings, both practical and theoretical, which survive in the biblical exegesis and moral exposition of the biblical commentaries, general guides to biblical interpretation, and studies of ancient Hebrew history and antiquities, and which taken together, as I have argued elsewhere, form a kind of received interpretation of Scripture. This essay, limiting itself to only a few major but interrelated themes, explores the *Vicar* primarily as a tale exemplifying the Christian's "progress of the soul" to interior detachment from the world, a progress through which the Vicar, as Goldsmith claims in the "Advertisement," stands out as "majestic in adversity."

I

The Vicar's use of commercial language and imagery to discuss morality and his children never reflects his own personal concern for wealth. His concerns, instead, as his worldly fortunes decline, focus on his family: "The loss of fortune to myself alone would have been trifling; the only uneasiness I felt was for my family, who were to be humble without an education to render them callous to contempt." His first attempt is to help the family adjust to their new, reduced circumstances: "My chief attention therefore was now to bring down the pride of my family to their circumstances; for I well knew that aspiring beggary is wretchedness itself." The Vicar's interest in sending Sophia and Olivia to London, in marrying Olivia to Squire Thornhill, and in establishing George in the army causes him to be blinded and duped by Squire Thornhill. But this interest hardly makes him a materialist, unless the honest promotion of a child's fortune somehow conflicts with morality or, as Hopkins continually implies, with a clerical calling. If, however, we recall the general financial plight of the lower clergy and their frequent and much discussed appeals for redress, the Vicar's disregard for his personal financial status reveals a model of clerical *contemptus mundi*.

The Vicar's language of the counting house derives not from a covert materialism but from the biblical tradition, however much it may have offended followers of Shaftesbury and those who believed the motive of virtue is its own reward. Eighteenth-century Christians recognized the commercial aspects of the Christian appeal to virtue, an appeal Christ himself made explicit often, particularly in his famous advice in Matthew 6:19–21: "Lay not up for yourselves treasures upon earth. . . . But lay up for yourselves treasures in heaven. . . . For where your treasure is, there will your heart be also." The commercial imagery of morality and salvation recurs again and again in the biblical criticism, and most forcefully in expositions of the parable of the talents in Matthew 25:14–30, a parable based on the metaphor of trade. Matthew Henry, perhaps the most famous biblical commentator, picking up on the metaphor, offers his own parable of the Christian as tradesman.

> A true Christian is a spiritual tradesman. Trades are called *mysteries,* and *without controversy great is the mystery of godliness*; it is a manufacture trade; there is something to be done by us upon our own hearts, and for the good of others. It is merchant-trade: things of less value to us are parted with for things of greater value. . . . A tradesman is one who, having made his trade his choice, and taken pains to learn it, makes it his business to follow it, lays out all he has for the advancement of it, makes all other affairs bend to it, and lives upon the gain of it. Thus does a true Christian act in the world of religion; we have no stock of our *own* to trade with, but trade as factors with our master's stock.

William Burkitt, whose *Expository Notes on the New Testament* went through an astounding number of editions, also saw the value of the trading metaphor, but he keeps it more submerged in his commentary on verses 14 and 15. The annotations to verses 16–18, however, give larger play to the trading metaphor.

> The former Verses gave an Account of the Lord's Distribution; these acquaint us with the Servants Negociation. Some traded with, and made Improvement of their Talents, others traded not at all; yet it is not said, they did embezzle their Talent, but not improve it. *Learn,* It is not sufficient to justify us, that we do not abuse our Talents; it is Fault enough to hide them, and not

improve them; the slothful Servant shall no more escape Punishment, than the wasteful Servant.

Like Burkitt, Philip Doddridge, in his widely known *Family Expositor*,
plays down the trading metaphor at first, focusing instead on diligence and
sloth. In the "Improvement" section of practical advice following the parable, however, he invokes it with full force as an incitement to virtue:
"What can excite us to a becoming care and activity in the duties of life, if
we are deaf to those various and important motives which this excellent
parable suggests? We have each of us received our talents, whether five, or
two, or one. . . . Our acceptance and reward will be proportionable to our
diligence." Later he exhorts, "Whatever our particular snares in life may be,
let us think of the doom of the slothful servant, to awaken our souls, and to
deter us from every degree of unfaithfulness." After a discussion of the
monetary value of a talent in Christ's time, John Gill, a secondary commentator, invokes the trading metaphor to describe the calling of a clergyman. Gill acknowledges that the talents stand for "the gifts of nature and of
providence," but he wants to focus on "ministerial gifts, such as fit and
qualify men to be preachers of the Gospel" (*An Exposition of the New
Testament*). Following this bent, he concludes: "The ministers of the Gospel
are traders, not in their own name, nor on their own stock, and for themselves, but for Christ, and for the good of immortal souls: they closely
attend unto, and work at, their business and employment." In effect, Gill
transfers Henry's general metaphor of the spiritual tradesmen to the clerical
calling, thus including the work of the clergy as part of the "business" of
life.

If the Vicar's "counting house" language for virtue reflects the eighteenth-century Christian tradition, so does his conception of his children as
supports for old age. The expositions of the various biblical texts referring
to children form a running gloss on the Vicar's attitude. Annotating Exodus
20:12 ("Honour thy father and thy mother"), Henry specifically points out
that children should endeavor "in every thing to be the comfort of their
parents, and to make their old age easy to them; maintaining them if they
stand in need of support, which our Saviour makes to be particularly intended in this Commandment, *Mat.* 15.4, 5, 6." These sentiments are echoed in Bishop Patrick's famous commentary on the Old Testament, and
Patrick also echoes Henry's exposition of the wish in Ruth 4:15 that David
become the nourisher of Naomi's old age: " 'Tis a great comfort to those
that are going into years, to see those that descend from them, growing up,
that are likely, by the blessing of God to be a stay, and support to them,

when the years come wherein they will need such." Commenting on Psalm 127:4 ("As arrows are in the hand of a mighty man; so are children of the youth"), Bishop Patrick writes: "And yet there is nothing of which we are more desirous than a numerous issue; . . . for they will be no less defence to us in our age, than arrows or darts are in the hand of a valiant champion, to beat off his assailants."

Bishop Patrick's reference to "numerous issue" points forward to Psalm 128, the next psalm, which, in verse 3, blesses the man who has a fruitful wife and who shall see his children like olive plants around his table. The Vicar is blessed with six children, and while he sees them as "supports of my declining age," he also, in the manner of Count Abensberg, who presented his children to Henry II "as the most valuable offering he had to bestow," considers them "a very valuable present made to my country." The Vicar's delight in his children clearly reflects Psalm 128, and Henry's exposition of verse 3, which connects the family circle with Job, may serve as a commentary on the Vicar and his family circle: " 'Tis pleasant to parents that have a table spread, tho' but with ordinary fare, to see their *children round about it*; To have many children, enough to *surround* it, and those *with them* and not scatter'd, or the parents forc'd upon them; *Job* makes it one of the first instances of his former prosperity, that *his children were about him*." The joys of children, Henry continues, are "To have them *at table*, to keep up the pleasantness of the table talk. To have them *in health*, craving food and not physic: To have them like *olive plants*, straight and green, sucking in the sap of their good education, and likely in due time to be serviceable." Henry's exposition here could serve as an outline of the first two chapters of the *Vicar*, and indeed suggests the Vicar's statement about his children: "My children, the offspring of temperance, as they were educated without softness, so they were at once well formed and healthy; my sons hardy and active, my daughters beautiful and blooming."

The Vicar's "commercial" view of virtue and his children accords with the eighteenth-century biblical tradition, but it does not acquit him of worldly attachment. The Vicar's frequent references to his children as treasures indicate he has indeed confused earthly treasure with treasure in heaven; he has substituted for heavenly treasure not wealth but an attachment to family. This pride of family appears blatantly in a statement the Vicar makes to his wife just moments before the announcement that Olivia has eloped with Squire Thornhill: " 'We are descended from ancestors that knew no stain, and we shall leave a good and virtuous race of children behind us.' " The various expositions of Matthew 6:19 clarify the Vicar's problem. Although they inevitably focus on wealth and material goods as the worldly treasure most tempting to men, they also make clear that any worldly attachment constitutes laying up one's treasure in this world instead of in the next. Burkitt argues "That every Man has his Treasure; and whatsoever or wheresoever that Treasure is it is attractive, and draws the Heart of Man unto it: For every Man's Treasure is his chief Good." The prohibition against laying up treasure on earth means to "take heed of an inordinate Affection to, of an excessive Pursuit after, of a vain Confidence and Trust in any earthly Comfort, as your Chief Treasure." Henry elaborates further: "Something or other every man has which he makes his *Treasure*, his portion, which his heart is upon, to which he carries all he can get, and which he depends upon for hereafter." The "forbidden" treasure, contends [Daniel] Whitby, is any worldly good "we chiefly prize, delight in, and set out heart upon . . . and which we do chiefly spend our time and study to pursue and prosecute, with the neglect or to the hazard of our heavenly treasure" (*Critical Commentary*).

The Vicar's pride of family reveals itself more obviously in his deference to his wife and daughters, even when he knows they are being vain and silly. The Vicar satirizes his wife and daughters regularly for their vanity and pretentiousness, sometimes to good effect, as when the shamed girls cut up the trains of their dresses to make clothes for the young boys, or when the Vicar spills the cosmetic wash into the fire. Most often, however, he capitulates, and every time he makes sure the reader knows he is aware now of his foolishness. He says, for example, that his wife's dismissal of Burchell as a match for one of the girls, because of his low birth and fortune, was in a "lofty strain" and a "delusion." Since such delusions "tend to make us more happy," the Vicar ignores them as harmless. But the Vicar retrospectively knows such delusions are not harmless, for he later discloses that they precipitate Olivia's elopement with Squire Thornhill. The Vicar finally joins his family in trusting the Squire, and at the same time reveals his foolishness in giving that trust. Before he is taken in by the Squire he receives warnings about the Squire's baseness and himself speaks against "disproportioned acquaintances," even giving the family "long and painful lectures upon temperance, simplicity, and contentment." The language he uses to describe his setting off for the fair indicates the Vicar now knows that as a man with only family experience, he should not have considered himself a match for men of the world: "Though this was one of the first mercantile transactions of my life, yet I had no doubt about acquitting myself with reputation. The opinion a man forms of his own prudence is measured by that of the company he keeps, and as mine was mostly in the family way, I had conceived no unfavourable sentiments of my worldly wisdom." When the Vicar remains "neuter" during the argument between his wife and Burchell, he is clearly deferring to his family, and he now admits it: "Our breach of hospitality went to my conscience a little: but I quickly silenced that monitor by two or three specious reasons, which served to satisfy and reconcile me to myself."

More importantly, however, the Vicar attempts to turn his family into a little paradise, where the closed family circle becomes a haven from the world, making a separate peace. In the opening chapter he writes: "We had no revolutions to fear, nor fatigues to undergo; all our adventures were by the fire-side, and all our migrations from the blue bed to the brown." For some years this closed family circle protected the Primroses from the major problems of life.

> Thus we lived several years in a state of much happiness, not but that we sometimes had those little rubs which Providence sends to enhance the value of its favours. My orchard was often robbed by school boys, and my wife's custards plundered by the cats or the children. The 'Squire would sometimes fall asleep in the most pathetic parts of my sermon, or his lady return my wife's civilities at church with a mutilated curtesy. But we soon got over the uneasiness caused by such accidents, and usually in three or four days began to wonder how they vext us.

As their three to four day vexation over trifles suggests, prior to his adversity the Vicar and his family, in Milton's famous terms, possess "a fugitive and cloistered virtue, unexercised and unbreathed, that never sallies out and sees her adversary, but slinks out of the race where that immortal garland is to be run for, not without dust and heat." This cloistered virtue extends throughout the whole family: "In short, a family likeness prevailed through all, and properly speaking, they had but one character, that of being all equally generous, credulous, simple, and inoffensive." By using the family circle as a protection against the world, the Vicar, again in Milton's terms, turns virtue into a "blank," for it "is but a youngling in the contemplation of evil, and knows not the utmost that vice promises to her followers, and rejects it." The Vicar's story, in good part, concerns the uncloistering of his virtue, its sallying out to meet the adversary, its contemplating evil and rejecting it. And at the heart of this new adventure lies the purging of his pride of family.

II

The Vicar's pride of family relates intimately to the much discussed prudence theme in the tale. Prudence is a complex term for Goldsmith, as it was for Fielding and Smollett, for it denominated both true and false prudence at the same time. True prudence, long held in the Christian tradition as the highest of the cardinal virtues, defines the practical wisdom that chooses right ends and the right means to achieve those ends. True prudence also implies the necessity for the Christian to protect himself, his proper self-interest, from the imposition of the vicious, to acquire enough worldly cunning or the wisdom of the serpent. False prudence, what the scholastics called "carnal" prudence, consists precisely in the cunning of the vicious or, at least, in the hypocrisy that promotes self-interest at the expense of others. True prudence equals "deceit in defense of virtue," while false prudence equals "deceit in defense of vice" or self-interest. In the tale, the Vicar satirizes himself for his deficiencies in true prudence, for often failing to guard against the imposition of the vicious. In terms of right means and ends, he is especially guilty, for his deference to his family's vanity certainly constitutes imprudence instead of making him the true law-giver to his "little republic" that he idealizes. The Vicar even accuses himself of false prudence when he claims that the family's social pretentiousness "in coping with our betters" comprises "attempts to impose upon the world."

The family's attempt to deceive Squire Thornhill with Olivia's pretended fondness for Farmer Williams comes dangerously close to a grave case of false prudence. It escapes that charge largely because the deceit is in defense of virtue. Although the Vicar worries that the scheme "had too much cunning to give me entire satisfaction," he agrees to it, "as our principal object was to discover the honour of Mr. Thornhill's address. " He, of course, also insists, and Olivia agrees, that she marry Farmer Williams, if Squire Thornhill fails to propose marriage. The Vicar's use of the term *cunning* suggests his nervousness about even true prudence—it too readily slips into false prudence. The danger is captured admirably in Hannah More's once popular verses, "Sensibility":

> And while Discretion all our views should guide,
> Beware, lest secret aims and ends she hide;
> Though midst the crowd of virtues, 'tis her part,
> Like a firm sentinel, to guard the heart;
> Beware, lest Prudence self become unjust,
> Who never was deceiv'd, I would not trust;

     Prudence must never be suspicion's slave,
     The world's wise man is more than half a knave.

The Vicar echoes the sentiment of the last line when his wife berates Moses for his failure at the fair. Mrs. Primrose cries, "The blockhead has been imposed upon, and should have known his company better." But the Vicar replies, " 'you are wrong, he should not have known them at all.' "

As the Vicar's last statement suggests the prudence theme in the *Vicar* is not primarily intended to demonstrate that the Christian needs true prudence to survive in the world. It rather demonstrates that neither true prudence nor false prudence guarantees a safeguard against imposition and deceit. It has not been often enough recalled, although some years ago Curtis Dahl pointed it out, that the Vicar is not the only one deceived in the story; everyone is at some time deceived—including the villains, and most especially Squire Thornhill, who is duped in the end by Jenkinson. Most importantly, even Sir William, who as Burchell roams the countryside as a benevolent misanthrope and prides himself on remaining benevolent while guarding against imposition, is so deceived by his own nephew that he must exclaim: " 'Heavens, . . . what a viper have I been fostering in my bosom.' " Burchell often serves as a satirist of the Vicar's deficiencies in true prudence, as in the famous "fudge" scene, but in the end, like the Vicar, he too suffers imposition. In this world of disguises neither true nor false prudence guarantees success; rather, both result in success and failure indiscriminately, as the Vicar suggests in the heading to chapter 28: "Happiness and misery rather the result of prudence than of virtue in this life. Temporal evils or felicities being regarded by heaven as things merely in themselves trifling and unworthy its care in the distribution." This chapter heading recalls the Vicar's statement after he learns the merchant has absconded with his money: " 'You can't be ignorant, my children,' cried I, 'that no prudence of ours could have prevented our late misfortune; but prudence may do much in disappointing its effects.' " The tale, however, ironically demonstrates that attempts to exercise true prudence, however praiseworthy, may result in events just as contrary to expectations as the actions of the Vicar's merchant. The irony doubles: no prudence of anyone in the tale helps to catch the merchant, thereby recovering the Vicar's money.

Instead of the moral virtue of prudence, the *Vicar* proposes a higher prudence, the religious prudence that St. Paul calls worldly folly: "Let no man deceive himself. If any man among you seemeth to be wise in this world, let him become a fool, that he may be wise. For the wisdom of this world is foolishness with God. For it is written, He taketh the wise in their

own craftiness" (1 Cor. 3:18–19). The various expositions of Paul's famous
Christian folly illuminate Goldsmith's intentions. Burkitt, for example,
claims, "If we compare Wit with Grace, Learning with Religion, a rational
Head with a gracious Heart, the latter infinitely transcends the former in the
Account of God. All the admired Wisdom of worldly men, is nothing but
contemptible Folly in the Esteem of God. The World's wise Man is God's
Fool." Burkitt's commentary points to the moral and religious superiority of
the Vicar's "gracious Heart" over his attempts to exercise true prudence; it
transcends his deficiencies in prudence.

Matthew Poole's commentary links the two kinds of prudence carefully, suggesting Goldsmith's direction.

> God accounteth that folly, which the world calleth wisdom. . . .
> the philosophers and wise men of the world propose the happi-
> ness of man as their end, which is indeed the true end which all
> men aim at. . . ; true wisdom directeth the best means in order to
> the best end. Whatsoever directeth not to the best end, or to
> what is not the best means in order to that end, is not wisdom
> but real folly; *worldly wisdom* neither directeth to the best end,
> for it looketh at no further happiness than that of this life, nor
> yet to the *best means*, and therefore is truly what God accounts
> it, foolishness.
>
> (*Annotations*)

As Poole indicates, from a Christian perspective, the best end of happiness
is heavenly, the next life, but the best means may constitute suffering and
oppression in this life. The Vicar possesses a good stock of religious prudence from the start of the tale. He exercises it first when he refuses to
deceive Dr. Wilmot about the loss of his fortune. The messenger cautions
the Vicar, "for, I suppose, your own prudence will enforce the necessity of
dissembling at least till your son has the young lady's fortune secure." But
the Vicar rejects this temptation to worldly wisdom, false prudence, in this
case: " 'Well,' returned I, 'if what you tell me be true, and if I am to be a
beggar, it shall never make me a rascal, or induce me to disavow my principles.' " The results are predictable: Dr. Wilmot breaks the engagement
between his daughter, Arabella, and the Vicar's son, George. The concluding lines of the scene focus on Wilmot's own prudence, the false prudence
of worldly wisdom: "Mr. Wilmot, who seemed before sufficiently inclined
to break off the match, was by this blow soon determined: one virtue he had
in perfection, which was prudence, too often the only one that is left us at
seventy-two." The Vicar's estimation of Wilmot receives confirmation later

from Sir William, who comments on the apparent loss of Arabella's marriage settlement to the Squire: " 'I must confess, Sir,' cried he, 'that your present disappointment does not entirely displease me. Your immoderate passion for wealth is now justly punished.' "

The Vicar must use up a large portion of his religious prudence when he refuses to acknowledge either the legality or the morality of Squire Thornhill's proposed marriage to Arabella Wilmot. Even the entreaties of his family prove to no avail. Instead the Vicar replies with an allusion to God's words to Job's friends: "ye have not spoken of me the thing that is right, as my servant Job hath" (Job 42:7). The Vicar's allusion occurs in the midst of an argument that focuses on suffering to uphold one's beliefs.

> "Why, my treasures," cried I, "why will you thus attempt to persuade me to the thing that is not right! My duty has taught me to forgive him; but my conscience will not permit me to approve. Would you have me applaud to the world what my heart must internally condemn? Would you have me tamely sit down and flatter our infamous betrayer; and to avoid a prison continually suffer the more galling bonds of mental confinement! No, never."

III

At this point in the story the Vicar does not know the extremity of his suffering, but it is clear that as his various misfortunes occur, they are designed, in part, to evoke greater reserves of religious prudence that will detach him from the world, break his family pride. This detachment is suggested at the time of the Vicar's first misfortune, the loss of his private income. As the family prepares to leave Wakefield, the Vicar writes: "The leaving a neighbourhood, in which we had enjoyed so many hours of tranquility, was not without a tear, which scarce fortitude itself could suppress." It is clear that the Vicar thinks of Wakefield as home, as the settled place of his family: "Besides, a journey of seventy miles to a family that had hitherto never been above ten from home, filled us with apprehension, and the cries of the poor, who followed us for some miles, contributed to encrease it." With these statements the Vicar initiates the idea of detaching the Christian from this world, especially from any notion that the Christian can be at "home" or "settle" here. The Vicar's physical departure from Wakefield begins to remind him that his life should be a spiritual pilgrimage whose destination is not this world but the next. He has, in fact, set in motion a complex of allusions to Hebrews 11:13–16: "These all died in faith, not having received the promises, but having seen them afar off, and were

persuaded of them, and embraced them, and confessed that they were
strangers and pilgrims on the earth. . . . But now they desire a better country, that is, an heavenly."

The strangers and pilgrims verses (along with other associated verses in
Hebrews) received extensive commentary and found their way into numerous works of religious and secular literature. They are especially appropriate for Goldsmith's tale, because their received interpretation invariably
focused on the Christian's detachment from this world. The Old Testament
saints serve as models to the Christian, explains Burkitt, for they were
strangers and pilgrims in

> outward Condition, wandering from Place to Place; so they were
> in Affection and Disposition, looking upon this World as their
> Pilgrimage, and Heaven as their Home and proper Country,
> because thence they are born; there lies their Inheritance, there
> are all their Kindred, there is their longest abode. Christians
> should not only account, but confess themselves Pilgrims, and
> discover it by their journeying and mending their Pace heaven-
> ward.

The Christian's proper home is heaven, for as Hebrews 13:14 continued the
strangers and pilgrims image, "here we have no continuing city, but we seek
one to come." Commenting on this verse, the biblical scholar John Marchant
writes, "Consider the words absolutely in themselves, and two things seem
to be intended by them. 1. That our Condition in this World is very uncertain and unsettled. . . . 2. It implies a Tendency to future Settling, and the
Hopes and Expectations we have of a happier Condition into which we
shall enter when we go out of this World" (*An Exposition on the Books of
the New Testament*).

If Christians seek to settle in this world, they will discover, according to
Burkitt, that the world "will not afford them a City of Rest, hardly a Place
of Refuge; they must therefore arise and depart, for this is not their Rest.
Learn, . . . that God has prepared a city of Rest for Believers, so it is their
Duty to seek and secure it, and continually endeavor the Attainment of it."
But seeking the city of rest, the heavenly settlement, may bring the Christian
many trials and afflictions, as Benjamin Keach points out:

> The spiritual Pilgrim is also exposed to many difficulties in his
> Journey Heaven-wards. Terrible Storms sometimes arise, Winds
> of Persecution and Temptation blow so hard, that he is scarce
> able to stand upon his legs. . . . He is often beset with Crosses

and Afflictions, that he is as a Man in the Mire, and can hardly get out.

(A Key to Open Scripture Metaphors)

As Burkitt, Keach concludes, "So the Godly are Strangers in this World. . . . Hence they are made sometimes a Gazing-stock to Men, by Reproaches and Afflictions. And how grievously have they been abused by the wicked Rabble of the Earth."

The Vicar recalls the received interpretation of the verses from Hebrews when his two young sons offer Burchell their bed. He commends their Christian attitude, suggesting Christ as the model stranger: " 'The greatest stranger in this world, was he that came to save it. He never had an house, as if willing to see what hospitality was left remaining amongst us.' " The Vicar's reference to hospitality also alludes to Hebrews 12:2 "Be not forgetful to entertain strangers, for thereby some have entertained angels unaware." The verse is appropriate for the tale expounded by Burkitt.

> Hospitality is a prescribed Duty, but this Part of it, to wit, the entertaining of Strangers, which was so great a Virtue in ancient Times, is now driven out of the World by the Wickedness of some, and by the Covetousness of others; few Strangers are worthy to receive Entertainment, and as few have Hearts to give it. . . . our Hearts ought to be always in a gracious Disposition towards such Duties as are attended with Difficulty or Charge.

Burchell's later role as benefactor to the Vicar and his family may also be foreshadowed in the second half of the verse from Hebrews referring to entertaining angels unaware. Burkitt again comments to the point: "By receiving Strangers, out of Faith in Christ and Love to God, we may receive precious Saints, and (which is more) some blessed Angel sent to keep them."

The association of Burchell with Christ may also, as Battestin notes, suggest he is some kind of redemption, if not Christ figure. The suggestion doubtless exists in the tale, but it is faint, for the force of the complex of allusions to Hebrews supports the theme that all Christians are imitators of Christ as strangers and pilgrims in this world. The final allusion, made by the Vicar just before he goes to prison, makes this clear.

> "Almost all men have been taught to call life a passage, and themselves the travellers. The similitude still may be improved when we observe that the good are joyful and serene, like travellers that are going towards home; the wicked but by intervals happy, like travellers that are going into exile."

The Vicar's improvement on the similitude, emphasizing home and exile, indicates, I think, that he is consciously thinking of the network of ideas presented in the commentaries on the various verses from Hebrews.

The complex of allusions to Hebrews and the evoked received interpretation also points directly to the Vicar's first true crisis with religious prudence. When Olivia elopes, the Vicar at first flies into a despairing rage: " 'all our earthly happiness is now over! Go, my children, go, and be miserable and infamous; for my heart is broken within me!' " The Vicar clearly worries about his family pride: " 'Had she but died! But she is gone, the honour of our family contaminated, and I must look for happiness in other worlds than here.' " This last sentence makes clear that the Vicar has tended to seek happiness in this world, that his treasure has not been totally in heaven but in his earthly family. Significantly for his gradual detachment from his earthly family, the Vicar a few sentences later refers to Olivia's elopement as "the first of our real misfortunes." Olivia's elopement shatters the family, but the Vicar hopes to find her a "repentant sinner" and return her to "this house and heart" (the Vicar alludes to the parable of the Lost Sheep in Luke 15:4–7). During his quest for Olivia the Vicar falls sick, and finally comes to see his sickness as a punishment for his pride: "My health and usual tranquility were almost restored, and I now condemned that pride which had made me refractory to the hand of correction." The Vicar does not here identify the kind of pride he means, but that he associates it with attachment to family becomes clear in prison.

The Vicar's rescue of Olivia leads him to think the old family ways can be restored. As if to remind him that his attachment to family must be completely broken, the Vicar arrives home from his quest only to have his house burst into flames before him. The Vicar saves his children, receiving a severe burn in the process, and continues to talk of his treasures: " 'Now,' cried I, holding up my children, 'now let the flames burn on, and all my possessions perish. Here they are, I have saved my treasure. Here, my dearest, here are our treasures, and we shall yet be happy.' " The fire destroys the family hearth, but the Vicar hopes to prevent the shattering of the family circle. He acknowledges that the " 'real hardships of life are now coming fast upon us,' " and yet he thinks the closed family circle can be restored, holding the world at bay: " 'If we live harmoniously together, we may yet be contented, as there are enough of us to shut out the censuring world, and keep each other in countenance.' "

The Vicar's hopes are again dashed when his debt to the Squire cannot be paid and he must go to prison. Yet even in prison he attempts to establish some semblance of the closed family circle, lodging his wife and daughters near the prison and keeping the boys with him in his cell. The supposed death of Olivia, occurring while the Vicar is in prison, directly connects his earlier mentioned pride with his family. The Vicar can now legitimately acknowledge Squire Thornhill's upcoming marriage to Arabella Wilmot and request the remission of his debt: " 'Heaven be praised,' replied I, 'there is no pride left me now, I should detest my own heart if I saw either pride or resentment lurking there.' " Squire Thornhill's refusal to remit the debt keeps the family in stasis, until once more hopes are dashed. George, for whose sake the Vicar had incurred his debt to the Squire, enters the prison, "all bloody, wounded and fettered with the heaviest irons." This apparent blast of his last hopes for restoring the family reduces the Vicar once again to the verge of despair: " 'My George! My George! and do I find thee thus. Wounded! Fettered! Is this thy happiness! Is this the manner you return to me! O that this sight could break my heart at once and let me die!' "

The Vicar tries to compose himself, but again recalls the shattering of the family circle: " 'But I am old, a very old man, and have lived to see this day. To see my children all untimely falling about me, while I continue a wretched survivor in the midst of the ruin! May all the curses that ever sunk a soul fall heavy upon the murderer of my children.' " George exhorts the Vicar, concluding with an appeal to fortitude: " 'But you have often charmed me with your lessons of fortitude, let me now, Sir, find them in your example.' "

The Vicar summons the last ounce of his religious prudence, and looking to a future state, detaches himself from this world: " 'And, my son, you shall find them. I am now raised above this world, and all the pleasures it can produce. From this moment I break from my heart all the ties that held it down to earth, and will prepare to fit us both for eternity.' " In this emotionally charged scene the Vicar seems truly to have purged himself of his pride of family. He immediately forgets the other members of the family and becomes instead the clergyman saving souls.

> "Yes, my son, I will point out the way, and my soul shall guide yours in the ascent, for we will take our flight together. I now see and am convinced you can expect no pardon here, and I can only exhort you to seek it at that greatest tribunal where we both shall shortly answer."

The Vicar's final detachment from the world associates him with the biblical figure of Job as expounded in the received interpretation. While Job was consistently treated as a pattern of patience in adversity, his various outbursts of anger also were seen as betraying a latent pride. As both

Battestin and Lehmann indicate, his suffering in adversity supposedly purged
his pride, making him also a pattern of humility. This humility, however,
was also read as detachment from the world. The expositions of Job shift
rapidly back and forth between Job's patience and his final humility. Henry
claims the Book of Job "presents us with a *great example of patience*, and
close adherence to God, in the midst of the sorest calamities." But at the
same time he argues, "In general, Job was a great sufferer, was emptied and
humbled, but in order to his greater glory." Job's example teaches the
Christian the meaning of suffering and affliction.

> A good man is happy, though he be afflicted, for, whatever he
> has lost, he has not lost his enjoyment of God, nor his title to
> heaven; nay, he is happy, *because* he is afflicted; correction is an
> evidence of his sonship, and a means of his sanctification; it
> mortifies his corruptions, weans his heart from the world, draws
> him nearer to God, brings him to his Bible, brings him to his
> knees.

The famous biblical scholar Jean Ostervald echoes Henry's sentiments. Job's
example shows how God uses affliction "to make us sensible of the Vanity
of this Life, and to wean us from the World" (*The Necessity and Usefulness
of Reading the Holy Scriptures*). We learn from the story "To give Glory to
God, as *Job* did; to humble our Selves before Him." The Book of Job,
according to Richard Grey, "was written to give a Lesson of *Patience* and
Humility to good Men under Affliction, in all Ages of the Church" (*An
Answer to Mr. Warburton's Remarks . . .*).

The Vicar's tale, like Job's, ends with a happy restoration in this world.
The concluding scene recalls the opening chapters, a family scene by the
fireside over which the Vicar presides, "according to my old custom." The
Vicar's "old custom" is renewed and the family restored, but the Vicar
himself has changed. This change does not receive dramatization in the very
brief conclusion, nor should it be anymore expected in the *Vicar* than in
Pilgrim's Progress or *Rasselas*. Goldsmith allows a few suggestions to suf-
fice. One indication occurs in the Vicar's description of George reentering
the prison cell after his freedom had been obtained by Sir William: "He now
therefore entered, handsomely drest in his regimentals, and, without vanity,
(for I am above it) he appeared as handsome a fellow as ever wore a military
dress." The phrase "I am above it" recalls his earlier confession, "I am now
raised above this world," and suggests the Vicar's self-mocking awareness
of his former pride of family.

A second indication of the Vicar's change comes from the debate over seating arrangements at the wedding dinner. This debate echoes Luke 14:8–10, where Christ urges guests at a wedding feast to take the lowest seats and rooms. In the received interpretation Christ's advice, in Henry's terms, "gives us a lesson of *humility*;" Christ "wou'd have us all learn" that "pride and ambition are disgraceful before men, for *whosoever exalteth himself, shall be abased*; but humility and self denial are really honourable, *he that humbleth himself, shall be exalted.*" The lesson in humility has been learned, for the Vicar and his company accept "with great approbation" George's proposal to dismiss precedence, having all "sit indiscriminately, every gentleman by his lady." The characters are still human, of course, as suggested in the comic notation that the Vicar's wife, expecting to carve at the head of the table, is "not perfectly satisfied."

The Vicar's new humility also appears when he asks Sir William's advice about the justice of accepting his son's release from the marriage settlement, promised before knowing the fortune stolen by his merchant would be returned. Finally, the last lines of the tale point to the Vicar's new life of interior detachment from the world. During his sermon in prison the Vicar had declared, "Though we should examine the whole world, we shall not find one man so happy as to have nothing left to wish for." The concluding lines of the tale echo these words: "I had nothing now on this side of the grave to wish for, all my cares were over, my pleasure was unspeakable. It now only remained that my gratitude in good fortune should exceed my former submission in adversity." The recollection of the prison sermon does not, I think, represent a slip-up on Goldsmith's part, as John Dussinger thinks. The additional words "on this side of the grave" make the meaning clear: the Vicar's experiences in adversity have taught him to enjoy and be grateful for the pleasures of this world when they occur, including his family. But they have also taught him to remove his "affections" from them, to keep himself from becoming attached to them as "earthly Comforts," remembering that his real treasure resides on the other side of the grave.

Chronology

<table>
<tr><td>1730?</td><td>Oliver Goldsmith born November 10, the fifth child of an Anglo-Irish clergyman, the Rev. Charles Goldsmith. Shortly afterwards the family moves to Lissoy, County Westmeath, Ireland.</td></tr>
<tr><td>ca. 1735–45</td><td>Attends schools at Lissoy, Elphin, Athlone, and Edgeworthstown.</td></tr>
<tr><td>1745</td><td>Admitted as sizar to Trinity College, Dublin.</td></tr>
<tr><td>1747</td><td>Father dies.</td></tr>
<tr><td>1749</td><td>Receives B.A. degree.</td></tr>
<tr><td>1750–54</td><td>Fails to obtain ordination in the Church. Tutor to a family in County Roscommon. Goes to Cork (planning to emigrate to America?) and to Dublin meaning to continue to London to study law, but instead studies medicine at the University of Edinburgh with financial assistance from relatives.</td></tr>
<tr><td>1754–55</td><td>Attends medical lectures at Leyden.</td></tr>
<tr><td>1755–56</td><td>Walks through Europe, from Flanders to Paris (possibly to study medicine there), then through Germany, Switzerland, and northern Italy, back to England through France. Settles in London.</td></tr>
<tr><td>1756–57</td><td>Works at various jobs: assistant to an apothecary, physician, perhaps proofreader in Samuel Richardson's printinghouse, and usher (assistant schoolmaster) at a boys' school in Surrey. Contributes articles to the *Monthly Review:* lodges with its editor and proprietor, Ralph Griffiths.</td></tr>
</table>

1758   Briefly returns to the Surrey school as its head. Publishes a translation of Jean Martheile's *Mémoires d'un Protestant*. Promised post as physician with the East India Company but when he does not also get a job as hospital mate on a ship to India, has no means to travel out to the job.

1759   Contributes to Tobias Smollett's *Critical Review*. Publishes *An Enquiry into the Present State of Polite Learning in Europe*. Now known as "Dr. Goldsmith," although there are no signs of his having taken his medical degree. Briefly publishes a periodical, *The Bee*. His growing literary acquaintances include Percy, Smollett, Murphy, Burke, Young, and Johnson.

1759–60   Contributes essays to the *Busy Body*, the *Weekly Magazine*, the *Royal Magazine*, and *Lady's Magazine*.

1760–61   Publishes his "Chinese Letters" in John Newbery's *Public Ledger*. Continues to write for various magazines. Probably meets Joshua Reynolds at this time.

1762   Collects the "Chinese Letters," publishing them as *The Citizen of the World; or, Letters from a Chinese Philosopher, Residing in London, to his Friends in the East*. Writes for *Lloyd's Evening Post*, then turns from journalism to compiling and hack-work for Newbery. Publishes *The Life of Richard Nash, of Bath, Esq.* Arrested for debt; to release him, Newbery and Johnson sell a third share in *The Vicar of Wakefield* to Collins, a Salisbury bookseller. Moves in with Newbery at Islington.

1764   One of the nine original members of The Club (together with Johnson, Reynolds, Burke, Garrick, etc.), where his presence is recorded by Boswell in his *Life of Samuel Johnson*. Publishes *An History of England in a Series of Letters from a Nobleman to his Son* and his poem *The Traveller, or a Prospect of Society*. Moves into lodgings in the Temple.

1765   Publishes *Essays by Mr. Goldsmith* and a private edition of *Edwin and Angelina*.

1766   Publishes *The Vicar of Wakefield* and an anthology, *Poems for Young Ladies*.

1767   Publishes *The Beauties of English Poesy*. Newbery dies.

1768   *The Good Natur'd Man* performed and published.

1769   Appointed Professor of Ancient History at the Royal Academy. Publishes *The Roman History*. Remains in debt despite considerable income as writer: continues to accept commissions for hack books.

1770   *The Deserted Village* published. Goes to Paris in the summer. Writes *The Haunch of Venison*, addressed to his friend Lord Clare.

1772   *Threnodia Augustalis* performed. Seriously ill with bladder infection.

1773   *She Stoops to Conquer* produced at Covent Garden. Completes the first volume of *Grecian History* and contributes to the *Westminster Magazine*.

1774   Dies in his lodgings in the Middle Temple, from kidney trouble and fever. *Retaliation, An History of the Earth and Animated Nature*, and the *Grecian History* posthumously published.

1776   Monument by Nollekens raised in Westminster Abbey with Johnson's epitaph on him as a man "who left scarcely any kind of writing untouched and who touched nothing that he did not adorn."

Contributors

HAROLD BLOOM, Sterling Professor of the Humanities at Yale University, is the author of *The Anxiety of Influence, Poetry and Repression,* and many other volumes of literary criticism. His forthcoming study, *Freud: Transference and Authority,* attempts a full-scale reading of all of Freud's major writings. A MacArthur Prize Fellow, he is general editor of five series of literary criticism published by Chelsea House. During 1987–88, he was appointed Charles Eliot Norton Professor of Poetry at Harvard University.

RONALD PAULSON is Professor of English at the Johns Hopkins University. His books include *Popular and Polite Art in the Age of Hogarth and Fielding, Literary Landscape: Turner and Constable, Book and Painting: Shakespeare, Milton, and the Bible,* and *Representations of Revolution.*

R. F. BRISSENDEN is the author of *Virtue in Distress: Studies in the Novel of Sentiment from Richardson to Sade* as well as editor of *The David Nichol Smith Seminar: Studies in the Eighteenth Century.*

WAYNE C. BOOTH, Distinguished Service Professor of English at the University of California, has written extensively on rhetoric and critical theory. His books include *The Rhetoric of Fiction* and *A Rhetoric of Irony.*

OLIVER W. FERGUSON is Professor of English at Duke University. Besides his work on Goldsmith, he has written a study of *Jonathan Swift and Ireland.*

ROGER LONSDALE has edited the *New Oxford Book of Eighteenth Century Verse, The Poems of Thomas Gray, William Collins, Oliver Goldsmith,* and *Dryden to Johnson.* He has written a literary biography of Charles Burney.

JAMES H. LEHMANN received an M. Phil. in English and a J.D. from Yale University before his early death in 1982.

167

CHARLES A. KNIGHT, author of *Clarissa: An Analysis* and articles on Goldsmith, is Professor of English at the University of Massachusetts in Boston.

C. C. BARFOOT is one of the editors of the *Dutch Quarterly Review of Anglo-American Letters* and has published several articles on Goldsmith's poetry, as well as *The Thread of Connection: Aspects of Fate in the Novels of Jane Austen and Others.*

PAT ROGERS has written extensively on English eighteenth-century literature and culture; his books include *The Augustan Vision, Grub Street: Studies in a Subculture,* and *Literary and Popular Culture in Eighteenth-Century England.*

BERNARD HARRIS has edited Jacobean and eighteenth-century dramas and coedited *Early Shakespeare.*

THOMAS R. PRESTON, Professor of English at the University of Wyoming, is the author of *Not in Timon's Manner: Feeling, Misanthropy, and Satire in Eighteenth-Century England.*

Bibliography

Bäckman, Sven. *This Singular Tale: A Study of* The Vicar of Wakefield *and Its Literary Background*. Lund: CWK Gleerup, 1971.

Barfoot, C. C. "*The Deserted Village:* Goldsmith's Moral Body." *Dutch Quarterly Review of Anglo-American Letters* 12 (1982): 213–35.

Battestin, Martin C. *The Providence of Wit*. Oxford: Oxford University Press, 1974.

Bligh, John. "Neglected Aspects of *The Vicar of Wakefield.*" *Dalhousie Review* 56 (1976): 103–11.

Bohm, Arnold. "From Politics to Aesthetics: Goldsmith's 'The Traveller' and Goethe's 'Der Wanderer.' " *The Germanic Review* 57 (1982): 138–42.

Bond, W. F., ed. *Eighteenth-Century Studies in Honor of Donald F. Hyde*. New York: Grolier Club, 1970.

Dahl, Curtis. "Patterns of Disguise in *The Vicar of Wakefield.*" *ELH* 25 (1958): 90–104.

Danziger, Marlies. *Oliver Goldsmith and Richard Brinsley Sheridan*. New York: Ungar, 1978.

Dircks, Richard. "The Genesis and Date of Goldsmith's *Retaliation.*" *Modern Philology* 75 (1977): 48–53.

Duncan, Jeffrey. "The Rural Ideal in Eighteenth-Century Fiction." *Studies in English Literature 1500–1900* 8 (1968): 517–35.

Durant, David. "*The Vicar of Wakefield* and the Sentimental Novel." *Studies in English Literature 1500–1900* 17, (1977): 477–91.

Dussinger, John. "Philanthropy and the Selfish Reader in Goldsmith's *Life of Nash.*" *Studies in Burke and His Times* 19, no. 3 (1978): 197–207.

———. "*The Vicar of Wakefield:* A 'Sickly Sensibility' and the Reward of Fortune." In *The Discourse of the Mind in Eighteenth-Century Fiction*, 148–72. The Hague: Mouton, 1974.

Emslie, Macdonald. *Goldsmith:* The Vicar of Wakefield. Studies in English Literature 9. London: Edward Arnold, 1963.

Eversole, Roger. "The Oratorical Design of *The Deserted Village.*" *English Language Notes* 4 (1966): 99–104.

Ferguson, O. W. "Dr. Primrose and Goldsmith's Clerical Ideal." *Philological Quarterly* 54 (1975): 322–32.

———. "Goldsmith." *The South Atlantic Quarterly* 66 (1967): 465–72.

———. "Goldsmith as Ironist." *Studies in Philology* 81 (1984): 212–28.

———. "Oliver Goldsmith: The Personality of the Essayist." *Philological Quarterly* 61 (1982): 179–92.

Forster, John. *The Life and Times of Oliver Goldsmith*. Rev. ed. London: Bickers & Son, 1877.

Fraser, G. S. "Johnson and Goldsmith: The Mid-Augustan Norm." *Essays and Studies* n.s. 23 (1970): 51–70.

Friedman, Arthur. "Aspects of Sentimentalism in Eighteenth-Century Literature." In *The Augustan Age: Essays Presented to Louis A. Landa,* edited by Henry Miller, Eric Rothstein, and G. S. Rousseau. Oxford: Oxford University Press, 1970.

Fussell, Paul. *The Rhetorical World of Augustan Humanism: Ethics and Imagery from Swift to Burke*. New York: Oxford University Press, 1969.

Ginger, John. *The Notable Man: The Life and Times of Oliver Goldsmith*. London: Hamish Hamilton, 1977.

Golden, Morris. "The Family Wanderer Theme in Goldsmith." *ELH* 25 (1958): 181–93.

———. "Goldsmith, *The Vicar of Wakefield,* and the Periodicals." *Journal of English and Germanic Philology* 76 (1977): 525–36.

Goldstein, Lawrence. "The Auburn Syndrome: Change and Loss in *The Deserted Village* and Wordsworth's Grasmere." *ELH* 40 (1973): 352–71.

Green, Mary Elizabeth. "Oliver Goldsmith and the Wisdom of the World." *Studies in Philology* 77 (1980): 202–12.

Hamlyn, Susan. "A New Source for the Plot of *She Stoops to Conquer.*" *Notes and Queries* 24 (1977): 278–79.

Heilman, Robert B. "The Sentimentalism of Goldsmith's *Good Natur'd Man.*" In *Studies for William A. Read,* edited by Nathaniel M. Caffee and Thomas A. Kirby, 237–53. Baton Rouge: Louisiana State University Press, 1940.

Helgerson, Richard. "The Two Worlds of Oliver Goldsmith." *Studies in English Literature 1500–1900* 13 (1973): 516–34.

Hopkins, Robert H. *The True Genius of Oliver Goldsmith*. Baltimore: The Johns Hopkins University Press, 1969.

Jaarsma, Richard J. "Biography as Tragedy: Fictive Skill in Oliver Goldsmith's *The Life of Richard Nash, Esq.*" *The Journal of Narrative Technique* 1 (1971): 15–29.

———. "Ethics in the Wasteland: Image and Structure in Goldsmith's *The Deserted Village.*" *Texas Studies in Literature and Language* 13 (1971): 447–59.

———. "Satire, Theme, and Structure in *The Traveller.*" *Tennessee Studies in Literature* 6 (1971): 46–66.

Kirk, Clara M. *Oliver Goldsmith*. New York: Twayne, 1967.

Kosok, Heinz, ed. *Studies in Anglo-Irish Literature*. Bonn: Bouvier, 1982.

Lucy, Sean, ed. *Goldsmith: The Gentle Master*. Cork: Cork University Press, 1984.

McCracken, David. "Goldsmith and the 'Natural Revolution of Things.' " *Journal of English and Germanic Philology* 78 (1979): 33–48.

Mahony, Robert. "Lyrical Antithesis: The Moral Style of *The Deserted Village.*" *Ariel* 8, no. 2 (1977): 33–47.

May, James. "Goldsmith's Theory of Composition: 'My heart dictates the whole.' " *Papers on Language and Literature* 15 (1979): 418–21.

Orwell, George. *"The Vicar of Wakefield."* In *Collected Essays, Journalism, and Letters of George Orwell*, 268–73. New York: Harcourt, Brace & World, 1968.

Quintana, Ricardo. *Oliver Goldsmith: A Georgian Study*. New York: Macmillan, 1967.

————. *"The Vicar of Wakefield*: The Problem of the Critical Approach." *Modern Philology* 71 (1973): 59–65.

Rousseau, G. S., ed. *Goldsmith: The Critical Heritage*. London and Boston: Routledge & Kegan Paul, 1974.

Sampson, H. Grant. "Comic Patterns in Goldsmith's Plays." *English Studies in Canada* 10 (1984): 36–49.

Storm, Leo F. "Conventional Ethics in Goldsmith's *The Traveller." Studies in English Literature 1500–1900* 17 (1977): 463–76.

————. "Literary Convention in Goldsmith's *Deserted Village." Huntington Library Quarterly* 33, no. 3 (1970): 243–56.

Swarbrick, Andrew, ed. *The Art of Oliver Goldsmith*. London: Vision, 1984.

Wardle, Ralph M. *Oliver Goldsmith*. Lawrence: University of Kansas Press, 1957.

Wibberly, Leonard. *The Good-Natured Man: A Portrait of Oliver Goldsmith*. New York: William Morrow, 1979.

Wills, Jack. *"The Deserted Village*, Ecclesiastes, and the Enlightenment." *Enlightenment Essays* nos. 3 & 4 (1973): 15–19.

Woods, Samuel. "The Goldsmith Problem." *Studies in Burke and His Times* 19, no. 1 (1978): 47–60.

Woolf, Virginia. "Oliver Goldsmith." In *The Captain's Death Bed & Other Essays*, 3–14. New York: Harcourt Brace Jovanovich, 1973.

Yearling, Elizabeth. "The Good-Natured Heroes of Cumberland, Goldsmith, and Sheridan." *The Modern Language Review* 67 (1972): 490–500.

Acknowledgments

"The Novel of Manners" by Ronald Paulson from *Satire and the Novel in Eighteenth-Century England* by Ronald Paulson, © 1967 by Yale University. Reprinted by permission of Yale University Press.

"The Sentimentality of *The Vicar of Wakefield*" (originally entitled "The Distressed and Virtuous Hero") by R. F. Brissenden from *Virtue in Distress: Studies in the Novel of Sentiment from Richardson to Sade* by R. F. Brissenden, © 1974 by R. F. Brissenden and R. L. Brissenden. Reprinted by permission of Macmillan, London and Basingstoke.

"The Self-Portraiture of Genius: *The Citizen of the World* and Critical Method" by Wayne C. Booth from *Modern Philology* 73, no. 4 (May 1976), © 1976 by the University of Chicago. Reprinted by permission of the University of Chicago Press.

"Anti-Sentimentalism in Goldsmith's *The Good Natur'd Man*: The Limits of Parody" by Oliver W. Ferguson from *The Dress of Words: Essays on Restoration and Eighteenth-Century Literature in Honor of Richmond P. Bond,* edited by Robert B. White, Jr., © 1978 by the University of Kansas Libraries. Reprinted by permission.

" 'A Garden, and a Grave': The Poetry of Oliver Goldsmith" by Roger Lonsdale from *The Author in His Work: Essays on a Problem in Criticism,* edited by Louis L. Martz and Aubrey Williams, © 1978 by Yale University. Reprinted by permission of Yale University Press.

"*The Vicar of Wakefield*: Goldsmith's Sublime, Oriental Job" by James H. Lehman from *ELH* 46, no. 1 (Spring 1979), © 1979 by The Johns Hopkins University Press, Baltimore/London. Reprinted by permission of the Johns Hopkins University Press.

"Ironic Loneliness: The Case of Goldsmith's Chinamen" by Charles A. Knight from *Journal of English and Germanic Philology* 82, no. 3 (July 1983), © 1983 by the Board of Trustees of the University of Illinois. Reprinted by permission of the University of Illinois Press.

"The Deserted Village: Goldsmith's Broken Circle" by C. C. Barfoot from *Dutch Quarterly Review of Anglo-American Letters* 13, no. 3 (1983), © 1983 by *Dutch Quarterly Review of Anglo-American Letters.* Reprinted by permission.

"The Dialectic of *The Traveller*" by Pat Rogers from *The Art of Oliver Goldsmith,* edited by Andrew Swarbrick, © 1984 by Vision Press Ltd. Reprinted by permission of Vision Press Ltd., and Barnes & Noble Books, Totowa, New Jersey.

"She Stoops to Conquer" (originally entitled "Goldsmith in the Theatre") by Bernard Harris from *The Art of Oliver Goldsmith,* edited by Andrew Swarbrick, © 1984 by Vision Press Ltd. Reprinted by permission of Vision Press Ltd., and Barnes & Noble Books, Totowa, New Jersey.

"The Uses of Adversity: Worldly Detachment and Heavenly Treasure in *The Vicar of Wakefield"* by Thomas R. Preston from *Studies in Philology* 81, no. 2 (Spring 1984), © 1984 by the University of North Carolina Press. Reprinted by permission of the publisher, the University of North Carolina Press.

Index

150, 151; Job's wife compared to, 80; resemblance to Mrs. Bennet of, 13

Primrose, Olivia (*The Vicar of Wakefield*), 14, 17, 84, 146, 152; abduction of, 78, 86–87; Lydia Bennet compared to, 13; eloping with Thornhill of, 149, 150, 158; supposed death of, 159

Prior, Sir James, 45–46, 50, 127–28

"Progress poem," 71

Progress of Poesy, The (Gray), 72

Prospect of Society, A, 57, 63. See also *The Traveller*

Providence of Wit, The (Battestin), 78–81, 89, 146, 157, 160

Psalms, Book of, 76, 149

Public Ledger, The (Newbery), 53–54, 94, 96, 102

Quick's Whim, 140

Quintana, Ricardo, 31; on *The Citizen of the World*, 95, 106–7; on *The Deserted Village*, 49; on *The Good Natur'd Man*, 37, 39, 40, 41, 42; on *The Traveller*, 128

Rasselas (Johnson), 160

Retaliation, 2

Reynolds, Sir Joshua, 64, 66, 82, 97

Rhetoric (Aristotle), 50

Richardson, Samuel, 7; his *Clarissa*, 8, 10, 12; his *Pamela*, 8

Richter, Melvin, 134

Roderick Random, The Adventures of (Smollett), 10

Romantic Sublime, The (Weiskel), 74

Rousseau, G. S., 37, 129

St. James's Chronicle, 45

Savage, Richard: *The Bastard*, 56, 57; *The Wanderer*, 129–30

Schapiro, Meyer, *Words and Pictures: On the Literal and the Symbolic in the Illustration of a Text*, 88

Schultens, Albrecht, 75–76

Scott, John, *Critical Essays*, 68–69

Seasons (Thomson), 126, 132, 133, 134, 135–37

"Sensibility" (More), 152–53

Shakespeare, William: his *All's Well That Ends Well*, 5; his *As You Like It*, 4, 5, 142; his *Henry VI*, 126; his *Midsummer Night's Dream*, 140, 141, 142

Sheridan, Richard Brinsley, 37

Sherlock, Bishop Thomas, 79

Smart, Christopher, 75

She Stoops to Conquer, 1, 2, 4–5, 6; allusions to Shakespeare in, 140, 141, 142; as attack on sentimental comedy, 37, 44, 47, 48; as comedy, 141, 142, 143, 144; Constance's role in, 142, 143; dramatic language in, 142–43; Hastings's role in, 140, 142, 143; Kate Hardcastle's role in, 4, 39, 42, 43, 142–43; as major farce, 4–5; Marlow's role in, 1, 39–40, 43, 140, 142, 143; Miss Neville's role in, 142, 143; Mr. Hardcastle's role in, 140, 142–43; Mrs. Hardcastle's role in, 1, 4–5, 143; parody in, 39–40, 41, 43; plot of, 140, 141–43; role of Diggory and Pimple in, 141; role of Marlow's father in, 42, 43; stereotypical writing in, 43; sources of, 140, 141; squire as "low" character, 142; Tony Lumpkin's role in, 1, 4–5, 6, 142, 143; use of antithesis in, 141–42

Smollett, Tobias, 10, 14; *The Adventures of Roderick Random*, 10; *The Expedition of Humphrey Clinker*, 7

Socrates, 91, 92

Solomon, Maynard, *Beethoven*, 105

Spectacle de la Nature (Pluche), 132

Spectator, The, 7, 95

Spenser, Edmund, "Garden of Adonis," 120

irony in, 10, 11, 82–83, 84;
Jenkinson's role in, 14, 153; meaning of "prudence" in, 79–80;
mixed genres in, 11, 14, 78, 146;
moral movement toward humility
and the sublime in, 82–83, 85–89;
Moses's role in, 80, 84, 85, 153;
parody in, 82, 84–85; pessimism
of, 17–19; pictorial imagery transformed by *framing* in, 83–88; plot
of, 13, 14; portrait scene in, 83,
86; precursor of *Pride and Prejudice,* 11–14; prison scene in, 83,
87–88; relevance of strangers and
pilgrims verses to, 155–58; revisionist criticism of, 145, 146; role
of Misses Skeggs and Blarney in,
14, 84; role of whores in, 14, 17,
84; sentimentality of, 15–19; social
pretentiousness shown in, 13, 14,
82, 150, 152; Sophia's role in, 12,
13, 146; stereotypical writing in,
42, 43; symbolism of enclosure in,
83, 84; true and false prudence in,

152–53; Wilmot's role in, 79–80,
154
Voltaire, 11, 130, 131
Vom Geist der ebraischen Poesie
(Herder), 75

Waiting for Godot (Beckett), 121
Wanderer, The (Savage), 129–30
Warburton, William, 79; Warburtonian
controversy, 79, 80
Wardle, Ralph M., 128
Wasserman, Earl, 80
Weiskel, Thomas, *The Romantic Sub-
lime,* 74
Whitby, Daniel, *Critical Commentary,*
150
Williams, Aubrey, 71
Windsor Forest (Pope), 128
*Words and Pictures: On the Literal and
the Symbolic in the Illustration of a
Text* (Schapiro), 88
Wordsworth, William, 65, 120–21
Word to the Wise, A (Kelly), 139